St. Margaret's Bay

AN HISTORICAL ALBUM

PEGGY'S COVE - HUBBARDS

Alfreda Withrow

 NIMBUS PUBLISHING LTD

FOUR EAST PUBLICATIONS

Nimbus Publishing Limited
373 Mackintosh Street
PO Box 9301, Station A
Halifax, NS B3K 5N5
(902) 455-4286

Four East Publications
PO Box 29, Tantallon, Halifax County
Nova Scotia   B0J 3J0

Design: Paul McCormick
Editor: Grayce Rogers
Cover photo: Dale Wilson

Canadian Cataloguing in Publication Data
Withrow, Alfreda.
St. Margaret's Bay
Includes bibliographical references and index.
1. St. Margarets Bay Region (N.S.—History.
2. St. Margarets Bay Region (N.S.)—Genealogy.   I. Title.

FC2345.S23W48 1997   971.6'22   C97-950131-8
F1039.S19W48 1997

Preface

Since the technique for producing them was first invented, old photographs have given us an insight into how people lived, dressed and travelled. Being able to visualize how our ancestors looked long ago, the types of homes they resided in, and the way the community was situated before we were born, can bring us enjoyment and pleasure. As time passes on, our grandchildren and those who will continue to come after us, will be fortunate to observe these changes in our history through pictures and mementos that hopefully, will be saved and protected for the benefit of future generations.

Fortunately, finding pictures for this book was not too difficult since they were collected by the St. Margaret's Bay Historical Society in 1985, during the Bicentennial Celebrations. Copies were recorded at the Public Archives of Nova Scotia for the benefit of the patrons.

I hope that you will enjoy looking back in time as you gaze at the old photographs and reminisce about familiar landmarks and the people who once resided in and around the Bay. The book tells a story of families and institutions that played an important part in the development of the St. Margaret's Bay area. Although many of those individuals have passed on or the buildings have been demolished, they will now never be forgotten.

Acknowledgements

I am grateful to many people for the help I received in putting this book together. I would like to express my sincerest thanks to those who helped in making this book possible. First to Richard Rogers, my publisher, who suggested that I do the book and for his patience in waiting for its completion. To my friend, Gary Meade, for offering advice and suggesting material which could be included. To the Public Archives of Nova Scotia for allowing the use of the St. Margaret's Bay Heritage Society photography collection and to Eric Boutilier-Brown, the photographer for reproducing the pictures. To my husband, Perry and my children, Yetta, Ross and Adam for their patience and understanding for the lack of attention they received while I was researching and writing the book, and finally to my mother, Viola Gordon, my biggest fan.

Table of Contents

CHAPTER ONE
In the Beginning

HENRY AND SUSAN
SACK, MI'KMAQ INDIANS,
WITH HISTORIAN HARRY
PIERS. CAMP NEAR ST.
MARGARET'S BAY. C.
1934

PANS

The history of St. Margaret's Bay spans approximately four hundred years. During the first 175 years there were no permanent settlers residing in the area. Only the Mi'kmaq would spend their summer months, fishing and hunting along the shores of the St. Margaret's Bay and then returning inland for the winter months. Over the years archaeological digs have unearthed arrow heads and other Native artifacts as proof that the Mi'kmaq did spend time around the Bay. Even during the early 1900s they continued to set up summer camps in the Bay area.

Several islands, coves, inlets and communities have been named after the areas where the Mi'kmaq were known to have camped. For example, in Glen Haven, Indian Point Road extends along a point of land that juts out into the Bay and leads to Big and Little Indian Islands. It is believed that there are Native grave sites on these islands. At the Head of St. Margaret's Bay, near Indian River, a Mi'kmaq family by the name of Bernard was issued a grant of land during the late 1700s, which was eventually sold.

A census was taken in 1752 with 35 names listed as temporary residents of the Bay. However, by 1785 we see a growth in population as the first settlers were offered land grants on the condition that they take up permanent residence. Some of the first permanent settlers of the Bay area were the children of Foreign Protestants who had received land grants in Lunenburg County in 1752. Many of these men were farmers and fishermen by trade who wanted to own land and provide food and shelter for their families. By moving to the Bay they were able to pass on land to their children, so they could build their homes and provide a living as farmers and fishermen for their families as well. As Joseph Howe travelled around the Bay in 1839 he published, in *The Novascotian,* his observations concerning this tradition: "the practice at the Bay, is to give to children at the period of life when they can turn it to most account what would be theirs [after the father died]".

During the same time period, there was another influx of Loyalist settlers from the United States. These settlers were granted land in return for their allegiance to the British Crown. In 1793, a poll tax assessment was recorded showing a total of 59 families residing in the St. Margaret's Bay area. However, this number had grown to a total of 506 people after another assessment was carried out in 1817.

It is around this time that the Bay area grew from being a settlement to a number of separate small communities, with the building of proper stores, churches, way stations and school-houses. This was a period of steady growth and development. By 1840 there were a total of 161 families living in the area. The years 1840 to 1845 saw the construction of the St. Margaret's Bay Road which began in Armdale and continued on to Chester, in Lunenburg County via the Head of St. Margaret's Bay.

In the 1840s, as a traveller rode his horse along this narrow, rugged road he would come upon numerous hills, where he could stop and see for miles. One such spot was named for the owner, John George Dauphinee, located in Head of St. Margaret's

Bay and still referred to as Dauphinee's Mountain. Before the overgrowth of trees, a person could climb to the top and see a magnificent view of the many islands, coves and inlets in St. Margaret's Bay.

In 1847 the Royal Western Mail Shore Line stage coach began its biweekly runs on Wednesday and Saturday, which continued until the early 1900s. At the turn of the 20th century a more modern mode of travel was introduced to the area as railroad tracks were laid along the south shore of Nova Scotia.

It was during the years 1890 to 1910 that St. Margaret's Bay enjoyed a period of prosperity, due to a second building boom. Numerous buildings were constructed, either to replace or add to an existing structure. The Halifax South Western Railway, which ran from Halifax to Yarmouth, was completed in 1905. This railroad company constructed three railway stations in St. Margaret's Bay and offered a service for both passengers and freight. The Bay was very busy during this time period with trains passing through several times a day.

As roads were developed and improved, people were able to travel from one community to the next. Gradually the outside world began to become more accessible, especially after the introduction of the automobile. As a result, interaction among the settlers became more frequent as they joined together to celebrate popular events, such as weddings, dances, fairs, auctions and church socials.

The communities around St. Margaret's Bay were originally developed as small fishing villages, which were once isolated and connected only by water. However, as the different modes of travel evolved, many changes began to take place. What once was a road joining together a number of small fishing villages, now looks like one very long residential highway with churches, schools, small businesses and modern homes visible as far as the eye can see. Today it is difficult to distinguish where one community ends and another begins. The scenery within the individual communities has undergone continuous change also, as trees were chopped down and land cleared for the building of houses, farms or businesses along with the roads and railroad tracks.

**VIEW OF MODESTY COVE
IN INDIAN HARBOUR.
c. 1920**

PANS

**VIEW OF HEAD OF ST.
MARGARET'S BAY FROM
JOHN GEORGE
DAUPHINEE'S MOUNTAIN.
c. 1890**

PANS

CHAPTER TWO
Churches and Cemeteries

Religion played an important part in the daily lives of those who first settled in St. Margaret's Bay, which is clearly indicated by the numerous churches located in the various communities. In the beginning, religious services were held in the homes or local schoolhouses. As the villages grew, one of the first structures to be erected was a place to worship. The church was the unifying force that administered to the spiritual and social needs of the different denominational religious groups.

The families who first settled here were originally Lutheran. Since it was difficult to find Lutheran ministers they had to settle for the Anglican ministers who were available to perform the different religious rites. However, it was not long before the Methodists, Baptists, Roman Catholics and Seventh Day Adventists had churches built in order to practice their own religious preferences.

The most prominent architectural style of the churches found in the Bay area was the popular "Meeting House" design. This simplistic design is a basic rectangular shape which resembles a small barn without decoration. Several of the churches were designed in the Gothic style, which is distinguished by decorative additions such as tall spires, rounded or pointed shaped windows and often some form of ornamentation. Sometimes both of these styles were combined to form a more unique structural design.

As one drives along the St. Margaret's Bay Road it is apparent that the majority of people who reside here are of the Anglican faith. Several Anglican churches were constructed over the last two hundred years of settlement. In the small community of French Village, St. Paul's Anglican Church was first built in 1824 and reconstructed on the same stone foundation in 1863.

Mr. William E. Brine, a merchant, donated the land required for the construction of this church on the condition that 'four square yards' be kept aside for his family's burial plot. A small cemetery is located in the front of St. Paul's Church. The churchyard has a commanding view of French Village Harbour.

Pioneer Cemetery which is the oldest cemetery in the area is situated nearby. It was designated in 1794 when the local settlers paid six pounds to James and Susanna Boutilier for one acre of land. This cemetery is no longer visible from the highway, since trees and brush have overgrown the 29 headstones which are still standing.

The settlers slowly built their homes further along the shore making it more and more difficult for them to attend church services in French Village, especially during the winter. The answer was to construct a church in Hackett's Cove. In 1840, a small chapel was erected on land donated by Jacob and Hannah Boutilier. About 60 men helped to raise the frame for St. Peter's Anglican Church with the women doing their part by cooking the meals. When the people of the community joined together to erect a building it often provided an opportunity for the neighbours to have a social gathering. As the years passed, more and more families settled in the area making the little chapel too small for the growing population. It became necessary for them to construct a larger building in 1870 which would accommodate the increased number of residents living in the area.

The present church was consecrated on November 6, 1872 on the same site as the little chapel. In 1930 a Norman bell tower was erected at the west door in memory of James Edward

Shatford and his wife Ann Lavinia (Garrison) Shatford. The entrance was moved to the right side of the facade so the tower would not cover the beautiful stained glass window which is called the "Rose Window". This type of window is characteristic of Gothic architecture from the 13th and 14th centuries in France. The window contains several symbols which represent Trinity, Unity and Eternity.

A cemetery surrounds the church with a very old headstone erected for Jannett McDonald who passed away in 1789. It is believed that Jannett was related to Flora McDonald, who was responsible for helping in the escape of Bonnie Prince Charlie after his defeat at the Battle of Culloden. As a fugitive he had taken refuge at the McDonald's home on the Island of Skye in Scotland. Jannett apparently had kept the sheets that Prince Charlie had slept in and made a request that when she died she would be buried in those sheets. Her son, Hugh McDonald, erected a headstone and carved the following inscription:

> Here lieth the body of Jannett McDonald who departed this life June 3rd, 1789 Aged 67 Years also, Mary, Daughter of Hugh and Christine McDonald who dep. 30th of Dec. 1789 aged 9 mos. Also Catherine McDonald who dep. 10 May 1791 aged 6 weeks. This stone is Erected by Hugh McDonald son of the said Jannett and is the first stone erected in St. Margaret's Bay

In 1845, John Martin Boutilier of Boutilier's Point and his wife, Catherine, sold a small piece of land to the Anglican Diocese for five shillings. A small chapel was constructed by the parishioners of Boutilier's Point. This was the first Anglican church to be erected on the opposite side of the Bay, thus making it easier for people on this side of the Bay to attend church services, since the nearest Anglican church was located at that time in French Village. On November 15th, 1845 the exterior of St. James Chapel was completed and the first service performed with about 200 people present. Contributions for the construction of the church came from some very prominent Halifax citizens, such as the Cogswell and Uniacke families. Many residents of the Bay area also played a role in the building of the St. James Anglican Church.

The residents of Peggy's Cove, a small fishing village located at the entrance to St. Margaret's Bay, had designated a

JOHN FRASER'S HEADSTONE IN ST. PETER'S CHURCH CEMETERY. C. 1995

A. Withrow

JANNETT MACDONALD HEADSTONE NEAR ST. PETER'S ANGLICAN CHURCH, HACKETT'S COVE. C. 1995

PANS

ST. PETER'S ANGLICAN
CHURCH, HACKETT'S
COVE. C. 1900

PANS

small piece of land for the building of an Anglican church in the early 1800s. However, it was not until a public meeting was held in December, 1847 that a decision was made to erect a chapel in

their community. Reverend John Stannage, who was originally from the United States, was instrumental in the building of this and several other churches in the Bay area. He convinced several prominent Halifax businessmen to give a donation towards the construction of this church. Since a schoolhouse had already been built on the land that had originally been chosen for the church, James Croucher donated a small lot of land next to his home. Unfortunately the small chapel burned down in 1884. By April 26th, 1885 St. John's Anglican Church was erected on the

PEGGY'S COVE VILLAGE SHOWING ST. JOHN'S ANGLICAN CHURCH. c. 1930

PANS

same site. Today this Gothic styled church has a tall spire which can be seen for miles. It is one of the first structures that tourists see as they drive along the highway on their way to Halifax.

Shortly after the first St. John's Anglican Chapel was constructed, residents in Hubbards were also in the process of erecting an Anglican church on their side of the Bay. The cornerstone for St. Luke's Anglican Church was laid in 1848 on land donated by Christopher Schwartz. The first service was held on July 14th, 1850. At this time Hubbards was part of the Parish of Chester, however by 1871 the parishioners of this area made a decision to separate from the Chester Parish and join with the St. Margaret's Bay Parish. This Anglican church was also constructed along Gothic lines with a tall steeple being added in 1870. Carillon bells were added to the steeple in 1956, in memory of J.D. Shatford's parents. Jefferson Davis Shatford was a prominent businessman who had made his fortune in the United States. He was responsible for providing the finances necessary for the construction of several important buildings located in the Hubbards area.

The next Anglican Church to be constructed was St. Margaret's Anglican Church. It is located in the Tantallon area and was completed by 1906. Until this time, the residents of the area had to travel to St. Paul's Anglican Church in French Village

ST. LUKE'S ANGLICAN CHURCH IN HUBBARDS. C. 1900

PANS

or to St. James Anglican Church in Boutilier's Point in order to attend church services. This was a seven to eight mile return trip by horse and buggy or even on foot for those people who wanted to attend services or social functions.

St. Margaret's Anglican Church, which was built by Mr. Alfred Worger of French Village, rang its bell for the first time on April 8th, 1907. Mr. Worger was also responsible for designing the church's furniture, except for the pews, which were made by Rhodes and Curry of Amherst, Nova Scotia. Lights were installed through the generosity of the Dauphinee family as a memorial to Mr. and Mrs. Isaac Dauphinee who had donated the land for the building of the church.

Approximately 100 years after the first Anglican church was built in the Bay area, St. George's Anglican Church was erected in 1923 to benefit those people who lived at the Head of St. Margaret's Bay. It was designed by W. Charles Harris, an architect who had been responsible for the architectural design of several churches constructed along the South Shore of Nova Scotia. Improvements were made to the church from 1953 to 1968 with the addition of a basement as well as the installation of lights.

In the mid-1900s, another Anglican church had to be constructed in Indian Harbour. Donations were received from

WHYNACHT'S COVE WITH ST. MARGARET'S ANGLICAN CHURCH IN BACKGROUND. C. 1910

PANS

members of the community as well as from people in the surrounding areas. Work began on St. Andrew's Anglican Church in May 1953. Leo Boutilier of Hackett's Cove acted as the foreman of the community of volunteers who erected the wooden structure with their own hands. The building is 45 feet long and 25 feet wide, with a tower built on the west end. The church seats approximately 100 people. It was dedicated on November 22, 1953, by the Rev. H. Corbin, Rector of St. Peter's Parish and it was consecrated on May 27, 1956.

The oldest church still standing in St. Margaret's Bay was constructed in 1821. A small wooden church was built in Glen Margaret (formerly Lower Ward) and was first referred to as the "Meeting House". Land for the Methodist church was purchased from John and Susan Fraser for five shillings and is situated on the edge of Fraser Lake. John Lambert was the builder, who along with members of the church, volunteered time in erecting the structure. By 1844, the church was called the Wesleyan-Methodist Church. In 1925, several religious de-

WILLIAM BLACK
MEMORIAL CHURCH,
GLEN MARGARET. 1995

A. Withrow

nominations joined together and the little meeting house became the property of the United Church of Canada. However, it wasn't until 1939 that the name was changed once again to the William Black Memorial Church.

As the communities continued to grow, it became necessary for a second Methodist church to be built in the Bay area. In 1897, another small meeting house was constructed and was eventually called St. Luke's United Church. The Hurshman family donated the land which was located across from their home on the Old School Road. This small chapel served the Methodist of Tantallon for many years, until the congregation grew too large for the building.

In 1965, a decision was made by the parishioners to construct a new church. The church was erected on the main highway, further down the road towards the Head of St. Margaret's Bay and not far from the French Village railway station. Ira Swallow donated the land necessary for the construction of the new church. This particular St. Luke's United Church has continued to serve the community for more than thirty years. Today the congregation is once more attempting to raise funds to build a third church or expand the existing structure.

Many of the residents who first moved to the Ingramport community at the turn of the century worked for the Lewis Miller Lumbering Company and were originally of the Lutheran faith. Mr. Miller donated land at the mouth of the Ingram River for the construction of a small wooden church. In 1915, Mr.

Strum, of Mahone Bay, was hired to build the Methodist Church. Money was raised by the members of the community through the organization of socials and other fund raising activities. The Methodists of St. Margaret's Bay also owned land at the Head of St. Margaret's Bay. They sold this piece of property and put the money towards the building of the church in Ingramport, which is called St. Andrew's/St. Mark's United Church.

Until the 1890s there were no churches in the Queensland community. Church services were still being held in the homes of residents such as Hezekiah Brigley. However, by 1892 the Methodists of this small village decided to build a church on land provided by Mr. Brigley. This small plain Gothic styled church was named St. Mark's United Church and it served the community for many years. In 1969 the congregation decided to join together with St. Andrew's United Church in Ingramport. The former church was used as a craft shop and then stood idle for awhile. After being sold several times the structure was renovated and today it is used as a private residence which now overlooks St. Margaret's Bay.

For many years, the only family of the Catholic faith residing in the Bay area was the Mahar family. Thomas Mahar, who had settled in Glen Margaret, decided to build a Catholic church for the sole benefit of his family. The St. Margaret's of Scotland Roman Catholic Church was erected in 1845, not far from Mr. Mahar's home. For many years the parish priests of Prospect would travel from Lakeside to Glen Margaret and on to

ST. MARGARET'S OF SCOTLAND ROMAN CATHOLIC CHURCH IN GLEN MARGARET. 1995

A. Withrow

Dover, through all kinds of weather conditions, to offer church services to the Mahar family.

The first building was demolished in 1945 since the Catholic congregation continued to grow and the small wooden structure became too small. The second church was constructed along the same lines architecturally. Both churches had cross crowned corner posts at the front; however, the first church had no steeple. By 1960, the congregation had grown to such large proportions that the church had to be enlarged.

The only other Catholic Church located in the St. Margaret's Bay area is located in Hubbards. Rev. Leo Day was the parish priest in Chester from 1940 to 1946. Under his leadership, St. Anthony's Roman Catholic Church was constructed during this time period. It was designed along a plain line but was distinguished by a small rounded dome crowning the roof. In 1952, the dome was removed and was replaced by a three-tiered structure surmounted by a cross.

In 1973, Rev. Lloyd O'Neill became the parish priest and was there when the decision was made to construct a larger building and demolish the old church. By 1978 a new church was erected measuring about 75 feet by 40 feet and standing on higher ground, behind the site of the original church.

Of interest to passersby, is a granite cross, standing in front of the church and bearing a bronze plaque. The memorial commemorates the finding of a medal, which had been worn by Maurice R. Sabourin, a Royal Canadian Air Force flight sergeant, who had perished in an aircraft accident. During the Second World War, in November 1943, his aircraft crashed and caught fire in nearby Northwest Cove, Lunenburg County. His medal was found unscathed after being in the fire for more than five hours. This medal became known as the "miraculous medal".

In 1814, the Baptist Association appointed Rev. Joseph Crandall and Samuel Bancroft to preach along the shores of St. Margaret's Bay. This was the beginning of the Baptist Home Mission and of Baptist activity around the Bay.

By 1843, a congregation had been organized in Indian Harbour, with approximately 25 members. The next step was to erect a church; however, it was not until 1862 that the Baptist group had its own meeting house. A small plain church was erected on land which was donated by Cyrus Covey and Christopher Allen. Originally the Baptist church was situated on

MEMORIAL STONE CROSS ERECTED IN HUBBARDS IN FRONT OF ST. ANTHONY'S ROMAN CATHOLIC CHURCH. 1995

A. Withrow

the main highway, but the road was rerouted when it was paved during the 1930s. Today the church is located at the end of a dirt lane and is no longer visible from the main road.

At the Head of St. Margaret's Bay, the Baptists who lived there had to travel to neighbouring communities to attend church services. Many of them gathered in private homes whenever a preacher came to the area. By 1876 the Baptists decided to build their own church at the Head of St. Margaret's Bay. Land for the church was donated by Joseph Fader and land for the Church's cemetery, which is located on Mason's Point Road, was a gift from Henry Fader. In 1951, renovations were made to the church which was moved to a concrete foundation. The money was raised through a fund raising campaign and the labour was donated. The interior was refinished, a furnace was installed and the structure was repainted. During the early 1980s the structure was once more given a facelift with vinyl siding being added to the exterior of the United Baptist Church.

In Seabright, the Baptists began to organize a mission in conjunction with the Baptists of Indian Harbour. In July 1833, a group of sixteen parishioners was formally organized into a church, under the leadership of Joseph Dimock, the pastor of Chester Baptist Church. Pastor Dimock was often assisted by two Hubley brothers, Jacob Sr. and Ferdinand Sr. who were Deacons in the church. It is recorded that in 1834, John Hubley Sr. and John Hubley Jr. sold two lots of land to the Baptist church. One was to be used for the building of a meeting house and the second lot was to be used as burial ground.

The first meeting house was constructed on the corner of the main highway and the Beech Hill Road. It served the area as the first Seabright Baptist Church and once the congregation had outgrown the small church, it was auctioned off in 1893 for fifty dollars to Anthony Hubley when the present church was erected.

It was not until 1890 that the Baptist congregation in Seabright was able to build a second church. Land was donated by Isaac Hubley to construct the Seabright United Baptist Church. This large Gothic styled structure has a steeply pitched roof with the steeple situated off to the side of the main building. It is very similar in style to the Baptist church located in Black Point.

As was the case in many other Bay communities, the Baptist of Black Point first assembled in various homes to worship and as their numbers grew, meetings had to be held in a larger building,

such as the schoolhouse. Even though times were hard during the mid 1800s, the Baptists' faith was important to them. The strength of their faith was obvious, because even though money was scarce they still supported the Baptist mission. Plans for the building of a church for the area were made when a building committee was formed on August 3rd, 1896. Land for the church was donated by Ephraim Hubley, with the building being completed in the fall of 1898 and dedicated on October 9th, 1898. This wooden structure was designed along the Gothic style with the entrance off to the side and crowned with a pointed steeple. The Black Point Baptist Church served the community for nearly 100 years, until it was closed for regular Sunday services in the fall of 1982.

A small wooden building which is located on Longards Road in Upper Tantallon was the first church erected in St. Margaret's Bay for the Seventh Day Adventists. In 1889, Levi Longard donated the land and with his sons was responsible for the building of the church. Today it stands boarded up, because by 1975 a decision was made by the congregation to build a larger, more modern church a little further up the road, on the main highway. Once again the Longard family donated the land and a new structure was built under the guidance of Elder David Crooks, with services beginning by January 10, 1976.

Religion played an important role in the lives of the first settlers of the Bay area and has continued to do so. People still worship in the churches and meet for socials as they raise funds

BLACK POINT COMMUNITY WITH BAPTIST CHURCH IN CENTRE. C. 1895

PANS

SEVENTH DAY ADVENTIST CHURCH, LONGARD ROAD, TANTALLON. 1995

A. Withrow

towards the upkeep of the present buildings. The significance of the history of many of the churches still standing has increased over the last ten years. The William Black Memorial Church in Glen Margaret is the first church to be given heritage status. A bronze plaque was presented to the church by the Provincial Heritage Department in 1994. Through this type of recognition many of our historical buildings will have a chance to be preserved for future generations.

CHAPTER THREE
Education

The first institutional structure in the community to be erected was often the local schoolhouse. This building would also serve as a gathering hall for many public functions.

As the communities around St. Margaret's Bay continued to prosper, schools were required to educate the many children living in the different villages. By 1823, there were four school districts: Peggy's Cove, Margaret's Bay East, Indian River and Hibbert's Cove School District. These schoolhouses were built and paid for by the parents and cost approximately 100 pounds a year to operate. This money helped to cover the teacher's salary and the upkeep of the building.

During the 1800s religion and education were interconnected. The ministers were responsible for the organization of education in their parishes. Ministers usually wanted the teacher they hired to be of the same religious denomination as the children, so that religion could be taught as part of the curriculum.

Eventually all the communities around the Bay had their own schoolhouse built, but only a few structures are still standing. One of the oldest schoolhouses still standing in the Bay area is in Peggy's Cove. The small wooden building was built on a little hill, in the middle of the village. The land it sits on was purchased from George Garrison and several other villagers, so that they could erect a church. However, the schoolhouse was built first and constructed on the church property in 1839. Children attended school in this building from 1839 until 1958. Today the school is privately owned.

In 1848 the first schoolhouse in Indian Harbour was erected about fifty yards north of where the Baptist Church is today. A hall that was built by the Good Templars served as a

**FARM LAND IN HEAD OF
ST. MARGARET'S BAY
NEAR TODD'S ISLAND.
C. 1950**

PANS

**ROAD WINDING THROUGH
BLACK POINT BEFORE
ROAD WAS PAVED. C.
1920**

PANS

schoolhouse for about twelve years, until another building was erected in 1891. A twelve-room schoolhouse was later built to accommodate the growing population of children in the surrounding villages. East St. Margaret's Consolidated School is still providing local children with their elementary education.

The community of Hackett's Cove built its first schoolhouse at the head of Boutilier's Cove in 1838. Twenty-eight years later they found it necessary to erect a second structure and then a third building in 1898. This particular building was used as a church hall for many years and donated to the church by Guy Dauphinee. In the nearby community of Glen Margaret, the children attended school in Hackett's Cove, since it was not until 1910 that this particular community had its first schoolhouse

constructed near the William Black Memorial Church. This building was destroyed by fire in 1968 and then rebuilt. Today it is used as a church hall.

The St. Margaret's Bay school district included the community of Seabright and records show that a small schoolhouse had been built there in 1828 with 31 pupils enrolled from the ages of four to fourteen. It had been constructed in the same vicinity as the Christian Youth Centre which was built in 1950 and at that time referred to as the Albert School.

On the border of French Village and Glen Haven, George Croucher sold to Halifax County a small piece of land for $45.00 so that a schoolhouse could be built. Mr. Al Worger and Abraham Burchell were responsible for the construction of the school. This building, which is located on what is now called the Old Halifax Road, was first called the Victoria School and it was used from 1906 to 1957. Approximately 74 children were enrolled at the school at one time, under the supervision of only one teacher. The St. Margaret's Royal Canadian Legion later owned the building until they sold it in 1965. Since then the building was remodelled and was turned into a private residence.

Upper Tantallon and Tantallon were once part of the community of French Village. Their first schoolhouse, which was constructed in 1810, was built on the same site where the

VICTORIA SCHOOL CLASS PICTURE, FRENCH VILLAGE. C. 1940

PANS

FORMER SCHOOLHOUSE IN FRENCH VILLAGE RESEMBLES A VERNACULAR-STYLE HOME. 1903

present St. Margaret's Anglican Church now stands. It was called Head Harbour School. By the mid-1800s the school was in such a state of disrepair that a new school was erected a little further along the highway. A third school was constructed in 1942 on the same site with an extension added during the 1960s. For years the school was referred to as the Lower Tantallon School and at one time was used as the hall for St. Margaret's Anglican Church.

HEAD HARBOUR SCHOOL STUDENTS, TANTALLON. 1896

Education **29**

Near the East River in Upper Tantallon, stood a school that was also built in the early 1800s, until it burned down in 1896. Many residents realized the importance of an education and quickly rebuilt another school on the same site. The second East River School was used until 1953 when the Upper Tantallon School was built to replace the second school. The building is located today on what is now called the Old School Road. For awhile it housed the offices of the Supervisors of the Western Subsystem of the Halifax County-Bedford District School Board

and a resource centre. Today it is privately owned and is used for many different activities.

Due to the many changes which are taking place within our public educational system private schools are becoming a way of the future. In September 1995, three teachers decided to open a private school located in this building and called it the Crossroads Primary School. Only grade primary was being taught the first year but more grades are being added as the need arises. Further along the highway in Tantallon, a junior high school was built in the early 1970s and then in the 1980s, a public elementary school was erected for children residing in the nearby communities.

Since the early 1800s, several small schoolhouses were built in the community of the Head of St. Margaret's Bay. In 1838, the first settlers of this village constructed a church-school which was called "Filleul's School", named after one of their ministers, Rev. Dr. P.J. Filleul. The building was situated on Mason's Point about a quarter of a mile from the road. A second school was erected where St. George's Anglican Church is situated today, near Schooner's Cove. Unfortunately this school was destroyed by fire in 1883. The next school was built in 1892 and was called

ST. JAMES SCHOOL CLASS PICTURE, HEAD OF ST. MARGARET'S BAY (SEE APPENDIX). 1939

PANS

**INGRAM RIVER
SCHOOLHOUSE IN
BOUTILIER'S POINT.
1900**

Gary Meade

St. James' School. In 1951, the school was demolished and replaced by a more modern two-room schoolhouse with a third room added the next year. At first grades primary to eleven were taught there, until the mid-1960s when grades nine to eleven were told they would have to travel to the City of Halifax for their high school education. Today, the school is called Head of St. Margaret's Bay School with only primary to three attending classes. Also at the Head of St. Margaret's Bay, on a hill across from the electrical generating plant a one-room schoolhouse was erected in 1920 for the children of the employees of the plant. As the number of children grew, another room and a bathroom were added to the building. During the 1960s, after it was no longer needed, it was used for storage until it was sold to the Christie family in 1974 and converted into a private home.

Often the number of pupils was very small, but this did not deter the parents from providing their children with an educa-

tion. In Boutilier's Point the first school, which was established in 1838, had only nine children from three families enrolled. It was located on the crest of a hill on Island View Drive. Another building was constructed during the late 1800s. By 1920, 74 students were enrolled in the school, which at that time was named the Ingram River School. A third school was built on the same site during the late 1940s and renamed Boutilier's Point School. Even though all grades were once taught there, today only grades four to six attend this particular school.

The first school to be built in Black Point was constructed in 1879. However, by 1907 it was necessary for the small community to erect a second schoolhouse which consisted of two rooms and was situated where the Black Point Fire Hall presently stands. In 1956 a four-room schoolhouse was built on the hill behind the fire station, but today it is used for community

HALF OF CLASS PICTURE FROM HUBBARDS COVE SCHOOL (SEE APPENDIX). 1914

PANS

activities, since the children of Black Point are now bussed to schools in other communities.

On November 30, 1832 the first school in the Hubbard's Cove area was built and named Hibbert's Cove School. It was situated where the Anchorage House and Cabins is located today, on the Shore Club Road. Thirty-one students were listed on the register, with Mr. Joseph P. Williams as the teacher. At some point a second school was built where the present school is located on the main highway. A third two-storey schoolhouse was built during the early 1900s on Schwartz Road and today, it has been divided into several apartments.

A fourth schoolhouse had to be constructed to accommodate the increasing number of children in the Hubbard's Cove community. In September 1948, the first section of the present-day school was built from the donations received from Alma Shatford. An extension was later added with money from a special trust fund that had been set up by a former member of the community. During the mid-1950s, John Davis Shatford, upon his death, left the community of Hubbards a large sum of money which was to be used for educational, religious and recreational purposes. At this time the name of the school was changed to Shatford Memorial School, in memory of Mr. Shatford's parents.

Long ago schoolhouses were usually built with only one or possibly two rooms, with a wood stove located in the middle of the building to provide warmth from the cold winters. Students were often responsible for keeping the wood stove burning and their schools clean and tidy. Those students who arrived early were fortunate to be able to sit near the wood stove, but sitting near the stove could sometimes be uncomfortable because of the heat. So the choice was to either sit close to the stove and be too hot or be seated several desks away and freeze.

Slates were used as notebooks for learning their letters and the students would often share reading material. The Bible was usually the first book from which the children learned to read. For awhile only those families that could afford to send their children to school were given an education, until the Freedom of Education Act was passed in 1864, giving all children the right to an education.

Photographs give us an insight into how differently the children dressed from today. If we look closely we can see that

some of the children could not afford shoes or did not like the discomfort of leather. The number of children attending the one-room schoolhouse under the supervision of one teacher, could range from ten to 75 pupils, depending on the size of the school districts.

HUBBARDS COVE HIGH SCHOOL COUNCIL IN 1959-60.

PANS

MEMBERS OF THE ISNOR FAMILY IN ROWBOAT NEAR MOSHER'S ISLAND. C. 1925

PANS

EISENHAUR FAMILY SAILING IN THE BAY IN HACKETT'S COVE. C. 1939

PANS

CHAPTER FOUR
Fishing

From the time the first pioneers had settled in St. Margaret's Bay, the ocean was of prime importance. Each family usually owned some type of boat. The different types of boats that could be seen at one time in the Bay were anything from canvas canoes to three-masted schooners. Small sailboats and rowboats were often seen in the Bay as a means of relaxation and fun and are still popular today.

Wooden boats were built or owned by several of the residents living in the Bay area such as the Dauphinee, Boutilier, Covey and Hubley families, to name a few. Before roads became available, schooners were loaded with freight for Halifax, with such items as fish, lumber, sheep, cattle and the occasional passengers. The boats would return with merchandise required by the settlers. Around 1840, one successful gentleman, Captain John Dauphney was said to own a fine farm and a very extensive fishing establishment at Hubbard's Cove. He was one of the first

LEO, ROBERT AND ROSS BOUTILIER IN A BOAT IN BOUTILIER'S COVE, HACKETT'S COVE. 1930

PANS

Fishing **37**

to export fish produce in his own vessels to such far away places as the West Indies.

Many of the rivers and coves in and around the Bay were well stocked with different types of edible fish. Not only were the fish a source of food but fishing also provided part of the family income. Atlantic salmon was once twenty-five cents a pound with salt cod less than two cents per pound after it was dried, split and delivered to market.

Lobster fishing has also been an important source of income. Thousands of pounds of lobster have been harvested over the years. Lobsters are fished with traps that were once made of lathes nailed to saplings, with funnel shaped nets at both ends. A lobster goes into the funnel shaped netting, which is located in the area of the trap called the kitchen, where the mackerel bait is placed to entice the lobster to enter the trap. Then it swims into

LAST BOAT TO BE BUILT ON SHORE BY M. KENNY IN FRENCH VILLAGE. C. 1925

PANS

the second section of the trap called the bedroom where it may fall asleep. However, when the lobster is ready to leave the trap, it is not able to swim back out because of the shape of the netting and the movement of the claws. Many lobster fishermen today use a more modern, square-shaped, metal lobster trap.

Fishermen would check their lobster traps each day, and then put their catch in a cage that would be anchored off the shore. About once a week a lobster sailing "smack" would come and take the lobsters to the factory. At the turn of the century there were several lobster factories in St. Margaret's Bay. Both Peggy's Cove and nearby Indian Harbour each had their own factories until lobster fishing slowly went into a decline.

There was a time when children around the Bay had to take lobster sandwiches to school for their lunch. Many of the children were embarrassed because it was considered to be a poor man's meal. Fishermen at one time, caught large numbers of lobsters a day and sold them for $1.50 per hundred. Today lobster prices vary but range around $3.99 to $8.99 per pound and lobster is considered to be a rich man's delicacy.

Long ago, fish were caught by different means depending on the type of fish you were catching. In the fall, a fisherman would use a hand line for catching codfish. A number of baited hooks would be attached to a fishing line and put in the water. Two hours later there could be 20 to 30 codfish, each weighing approximately 20 pounds, caught on the hooks. The fishermen would split and salt these fish for the winter. The fish would be dried on flakes in the spring. Flakes were poles nailed to stakes about four feet long and covered with lathes. This method of fishing is still being used today, but the fish are not as plentiful or as large as they once were.

Fishermen still fish for mackerel, tuna and once in awhile they will catch swordfish. Tuna fishing has improved over the last two decades after a decline during the early 1970s. Today, fishermen catch, ranch and sell the tuna to different places around the world. Japan is the largest buyer of tuna. Fish plants,

A SCENE SHOWING BOUTILIER'S COVE IN HACKETT'S COVE. C. 1960

PANS

FISHERMEN ON BURCHELL'S WHARF IN FRENCH VILLAGE. 1935

PANS

buyers, computerized monitoring companies, inspectors and the tourist industry are the ones who benefit from this type of fishing.

Different means of fish farming are constantly being developed. Aquaculture has been a successful venture in St. Margaret's Bay. Mackerel trap moorings are left out all winter so that mussel seeds or spats can be collected. The fisherman takes the spats and places them into long plastic mono netting called socks which are obtained from the Department of Fisheries. A long plastic tube is placed inside the sock and the mussels are put down the tube. The tube is removed so the mussels can attach themselves to the netting. The socks are then returned to the salt water so they can grow for 18 to 24 months longer. This is a much shorter growing period compared to that of wild mussels which take about five years. A fisherman sets out about 170 collectors which are eight feet long and attached to long lines that have buoys to help support the growing weight of the mussels and to also show the fishermen where they are located.

Boats and the methods of fishing have constantly been changing over the years. Wooden sailing ships have given way to engine powered cape-islanders which are equipped with radar, depth sounders and two-way radios. Bank schooners were built for offshore fishing since they would be gone for weeks at a time fishing to the Grand Banks of Newfoundland.

At one time, former fishermen, such as Josh and Ben Dauphinee of Glen Haven had coaster schooners, which fished inshore and were gone only for one or two days. Today fishing boats that are fully equipped with modern technology as well as with their nets, ropes, anchors and floats can cost as much as one hundred thousand dollars or more. At one time nets were knitted by the fishermen themselves whereas today they can be purchased ready made. However, nets do have to be mended at times and this task is still done by the fishermen.

The current fishing industry does have other problems besides the decline in the number of fish available. Most fishermen are retirement age and the younger men who wish to pursue fishing as their livelihood are finding it difficult to start a fishing business.

Not only are the expenses, such as a boat, equipment, license to fish, enough to deter the young people from becoming involved in the fishing industry, there is also the matter of the amount of fish that can be caught by each fisherman. Even if a

MANUEL FAMILY'S FISH STORE AND HOUSE IN PEGGY'S COVE. C. 1920
PANS

person can afford to become involved in the fishing industry, there are no guarantees that they would be allowed to fish. In the past there were few if any government regulations, whereas today there are a number of rules that the fishermen must follow. They are now told how much they can catch and where and when they can fish. Heavy fines have to be paid if any of these quotas or regulations are broken.

For awhile there has been a steady decline in the fishing industry and as a consequence many fishermen are now out of work. Fishing sheds and wharves that are no longer in use are left to the elements and have been going to ruin. In Peggy's Cove, there are two structures that have been standing since 1814 on the rocks of the Peggy's Cove harbour. These two buildings have been constantly photographed and painted by numerous artists. Around 1993, the fish store and house, which are owned by the Manuel family, became registered as a Provincial Heritage Property by the Nova Scotia government. The buildings will be maintained by the government so that future generations will have the opportunity to see how fishermen in the past took care of their equipment and stored their catch.

HAROLD DAUPHINEE'S
PORTABLE SAW MILL -
CUTTING LUMBER AT
HEAD OF ST.
MARGARET'S BAY. C.
1940

PANS

CHAPTER FIVE
Lumbering Industry

It is difficult to imagine that long ago, trees were in abundance in the Bay area, even down to the shoreline. The first settlers would cut down only enough trees to build their houses, barns and storage sheds. Eventually with the decline in the fishing industry new industries had to be pursued as a source of income. Lumbering began to play an important role in the development of the St. Margaret's Bay communities.

It was during the late 1800s that the fishing industry began to decline causing starvation and hardship. Some of the inhab-

BYRON DAUPHINEE'S MODEL T, AND CUTTING WOOD WITH A PORTABLE CHAIN SAW IN GLEN HAVEN. C. 1920

PANS

itants decided to erect sawmills hoping to begin a prosperous lumbering business. There were several different types of sawmills set up around the Bay by families who in the past were fishermen or farmers. Portable as well as stationary sawmills became available in the St. Margaret's Bay area. The portable sawmills were used for small jobs and were moved to where small stands of lumber were piled. All mills did contain the same cutting saws so that they could cut lumber, laths, staves, boxwood, shingles and groove 'n' tongue boards. The mills also supplied necessary farm equipment such as dairy-farm buckets, tubs for shipping lard and trays for packing butter. Barrels were made of hardwood by coopers and furniture was built from the wood supplied by the mills.

Large sawmills could be found in a number of the communities, mainly where the different rivers flowed into the Bay. Over the years a succession of lumber mills were operated in the Seabright area. About half a mile up the Wooden's River, Steven Dauphinee built a mill which was run by a water wheel. Later it was dismantled and parts of the equipment were used to help erect another mill which was steam powered, near the mouth of the river. This mill changed hands several times and was known as Hubley-MacDonald Mill and the Roy Boutilier Mill.

As we continue around the Bay, a number of mills could be found in operation during the latter part of the 19th century and during the early 1900s. Tan Dauphinee operated a sawmill on Frost Fish Cove, out on Connolly's Point in Glen Haven. Nathan Dauphinee built a sawmill in Tantallon. Daniel Mason as well as John George Dauphinee each operated a mill on Fader's Point (now called Allan Heights). Oliver Dauphinee ran a mill in Boutilier's Point and the Shankel family operated a mill situated behind the family home in Hubbards. There were many sawmills which are not mentioned here that were in operation until either the forests became depleted or for some unknown reason the mill itself burned down.

There were several lumbering mills in the St. Margaret's Bay area that deserve special mention because of the part they played in providing employment. James Slauenwhite and his brother operated a mill in Tantallon, on Whynacht's Point as well at Stillwater Lake in Hammonds Plains and at Little East River in Tantallon. This particular mill was a steam mill but since the river had enough current, he changed it to a water

TAN DAUPHINEE'S SAWMILL ON FROST FISH COVE, CONNOLLY'S POINT, GLEN HAVEN. C. 1918

PANS

powered mill. Mr. Slauenwhite's sons played a role in the operation of the different sawmills. It was quite common for family members to take part in the running of the mills. They would be taught to carry out the different jobs required for operating a mill, such as firing the boilers, hauling logs and sawing the laths.

As early as 1872, advertisements could be found in the *Morning Chronicle*, a Halifax newspaper, offering the manufacturing of hemlock, spruce, pine and hardwood lumber sawn to the necessary specifications, with lumber planed and laths and boxes always available at the mills. Todd, Polley and Company, which was located on an island in the community of the Head of St. Margaret's Bay operated a prosperous lumbering company for a number of years. Today the island, which is still referred to as Todd's Island, is joined to the mainland by a small causeway which had been built by the lumber company. It had secured the rights from the Nova Scotia government to build a mill which operated on a marine engine and two boilers. By 1890, the company was sold to the Bowater Mersey Paper Company. Sawdust accumulation can still be found on the island as evidence of the site of the sawmill.

The largest lumbering operation to take place in the St. Margaret's Bay area was located at Ingramport. Around 1900, Lewis Miller and Company erected a sawmill which employed

**TODD & POLLEY'S
LUMBER COMPANY ON
TODD'S ISLAND
(FORMERLY CALLED
SHEEP'S ISLAND). C.
1880**

PANS

**LEWIS MILLER LUMBER
CAMP, MAIN STREET IN
INGRAMPORT. 1915**

PANS

**WINTER LUMBER CAMP
ON INGRAM RIVER. LEFT
TO RIGHT: JOE HANSON,
CARL JOHNSON AND
TRACEY BOUTILIER.
1925**

PANS

more than 200 men year round. From the spring until the fall the mill sawed 200,000 feet of lumber a day. In the winter the men would cut the logs. In the spring they would drive the logs 25-30 miles down the Ingram River to the mill.

Lewis Miller and Company was instrumental in the community of Ingramport for almost forty years. Mr. Miller hired a number of Swedish immigrants as well as residents of the Bay area to operate the mill. Homes were built for the workmen, with a large general store which was operated by the Young Brothers.

LEWIS MILLER LUMBER COMPANY GENERAL STORE AT INGRAMPORT. c. 1920

PANS

TWO LUMBERMEN BOXING IN LEWIS MILLER LUMBER CAMP IN INGRAMPORT. 1925

PANS

A church was also constructed for the benefit of the people of this community. These self-contained communities would also provide their own form of entertainment such as boxing matches among the lumbermen.

Large vessels would dock at the Miller wharves and load shipments of lumber which were transported around the world. The docks extended some 1000 to 1200 feet from the north to the south along the water shoreline, with the depth of water varying from 30 to 36 feet, providing one of the best loading places for ships up to five thousand tons.

In 1912, a newspaper recorded that during the year a number of vessels, which included schooners, barques, barquantines and steam ships carried away up to 12 million feet of lumber to ports in England, United States and South America. Unfortunately, in August 1928, there was a great fire which destroyed the general store, warehouse, two barns, seven houses, the cookhouse and the lumber yard. Thousands of feet of lumber were lost. Since the bottom was beginning to drop out of the lumber market, Lewis Miller and Company was not rebuilt.

CHAPTER SIX

Tourism

Even in the late 1780s, tourism was beginning to grow as a new business opportunity in St. Margaret's Bay. The first community to benefit from this new venture was at the Head of St. Margaret's Bay. George Mason built a house not far from the Indian River where sportsmen would stay when they came to hunt and fish. His son, Martin Mason, enlarged the house to accommodate the gentlemen who had travelled here for fun and relaxation. The house became known as the Fishermen's Cottage and was later called Will's Cottage. During this period, it was the only facility available for miles for travellers to obtain food and shelter. As the area became more and more popular as

HAYMAKING AT BLACK POINT. C. 1900
PANS

It's summer time at

BLACK POINT
N. S.

Headquarters for fresh air and sunshine.

a vacation retreat the cottage became too small to cope with the growing number of sportsmen and tourists.

Martin Mason saw an opportunity to increase his business so he constructed a new hotel. The Mason family opened for business July 29th, 1872, the Prince of Wales Hotel, which was named for Edward, who was Prince of Wales at the time of its construction. The building was three storeys high, with a mansard roof and 17 bedrooms that could accommodate up to 30 guests at one time. From 1872 until 1939, the King's Mail Coaches travelled from Halifax along the South Shore and stopped at the Hotel. It became a popular stopover between Halifax and Chester.

An advertisement was published in the *Morning Chronicle* in 1872 to let people know that the Prince of Wales Hotel was offering such activities as bathing, fishing and hunting for its guests. It also stated that the hotel had water throughout the house and bathrooms which in the late 1800s were considered a luxury. The hotel had several owners besides the Mason family until it caught fire and burned to the ground in March 1939. The hotel was not rebuilt. By this time there were a number of other popular hotels established in several communities. It was now easier to travel down the shore since more people were beginning to own cars and vacationers could visit the Bay by travelling on the Halifax South-Western Railway.

Another hotel worth mentioning still stands today but is now vacant. In 1903, Anthony Hubley decided to build the Seabright Hotel, which overlooks the St. Margaret's Bay. It is located at the end of Anthony Hubley Road and is no longer visible from the main highway. At one time, the hotel was one of the largest buildings constructed in the Bay area. The stones for the foundation were split out of the granite found further down the road in Indian Harbour. They were brought to Seabright by ox-cart and put in place, then held together with mortar that was made out of lime, sand and horsehair.

Lumber for the structure was purchased from the Lewis Miller Lumber Company for five dollars a thousand board feet and transported across the Bay. This wooden structure was once three storeys high with a gambrel roof and dormers. The hotel had its own tennis courts and a special canopy wagon would travel to French Village train station to pick up guests. A number

SEABRIGHT HOTEL AT THE END OF ANTHONY HUBLEY ROAD. c. 1915

PANS

of famous visitors such as Zane Grey and Franklin Roosevelt Junior stayed at the hotel to spend their summer holidays.

During the Second World War, this hotel played a part in housing a few navy men who required shelter for a night. Bad weather forced them to make an emergency landing in the St. Margaret's Bay. In January 1942, an American navy twin-engine patrol plane left Argentia, Newfoundland and was flying to Quoinset Point, Rhode Island. The weather was very foggy all along the Atlantic shoreline. Since the plane was a PBY-5 flying boat it had no wheels, so the crew had to land on water. The navigator of the plane made a decision to land in St. Margaret's Bay. The friendly people of the Bay went out in their boats to pick up the men. Some of the crew decided to stay on the plane while several others spent the night at the Seabright Hotel.

EMERGENCY LANDING BY AMERICAN AIRMEN NEAR SEABRIGHT HOTEL. C. 1942

PANS

The small community of Hubbards was also a very popular tourist spot with a few beautiful hotels of its own. The first hotel was built in 1853, by Charles McLean. The McLean's Hotel was used as a stopover for the stagecoaches which travelled from Halifax to Lunenburg. For more than 100 years this hotel was popular with vacationers looking for enjoyment and relaxation. In 1966, the government purchased the building and had it demolished. A post office now stands on the site of the former hotel.

Across the cove, opposite the MacLean's Hotel, another hotel was built to accommodate the increase of visitors to the Hubbards area. During the latter part of the 1800s, David Dauphinee built the Dauphinee Hotel on a piece of land called Dauphinee's Point. It resembled a large house until his son Henry added a three storey extension in 1905. Unfortunately this structure caught fire and was destroyed in the early 1930s.

HENRY DAUPHINEE'S HOTEL ON DAUPHINEE'S POINT IN HUBBARDS. C. 1915

Next door to the MacLean's Hotel, A.W. Shatford decided to construct a beautiful hotel in 1884. The Gainsborough Hotel was three-and-one-half storeys high with two open verandahs extending across the facade of the building. This hotel offered a number of popular activities for its guests such as canoeing, swimming, sailing, rowing, tennis and shuffleboard.

Once the tourist trade in Hubbards began to decline the Gainsborough Hotel was sold in 1944 to the government. The government had already built the St. Margaret's Bay Training School for the Merchant Marines behind the hotel. Now the hotel would accommodate the officers, offices and a mess hall with barracks built behind the hotel to house the cadets and

seamen. However, not long after the changes were put in place the Second World War ended and the hotel was no longer needed. Unfortunately, the beautiful structure was left empty for awhile. A number of business ventures took over the facility for several years. The hotel, along with the buildings surrounding it, was used as a Missionary Bible Institute, margarine factory, and a fish chowder factory. The government attempted to find a use for the old hotel but eventually the decision to demolish the historical landmark was made in 1968. A library was constructed on the site.

In 1905, the Iona Hotel was built by William Allen of New York City. This structure is still standing on the Shore Club Road and is now called the Dauphinee Inn. During the late 1800s many of the young women of the Bay area could not find work, so they would move to the United States in hopes of obtaining employment as domestics. Sadie Dauphinee travelled to New York City and was employed by the Allen family. After Mr. Allen's wife passed away he fell in love and married his housekeeper, Sadie. When Mr. Allen's health began to deteriorate, they made the decision to move to Sadie's hometown of Hubbards.

William Allen built the Iona Hotel along the same design as their home on Park Avenue in the city of New York. Since Mr. Allen was a man of means the building was one of the first structures in Hubbards to have gas lights installed. Approximately eleven years after he built the hotel, Mr. Allen passed away and Sadie lived there until her death in 1927.

DAUPHINEE'S INN IN HUBBARDS BUILT IN 1905 BY WILLIAM ALLEN. 1995

A. Withrow

QUEENSLAND BEACH, HUBBARDS, N.S.

The Iona Hotel has been sold several times since the Allens passed away and has changed its name several times over the years. When it was purchased by the Harnish family in the early 1990s they renamed it the Dauphinee Inn. The present owners, Rhys and Kim Harnish, have honoured many of the families living in the Hubbards area by naming the rooms within the inn after the pioneers who first settled in the community.

A VIEW OF QUEENSLAND BEACH - A POPULAR SWIMMING SPOT. C. 1927

PANS

**A MOTOR BOAT PARTY IN
HUBBARD'S COVE NEAR
DAUPHINEE'S POINT. C.
1915**

PANS

Since the decline of the fishing and lumbering industries tourism has continued to grow as the main source of income. Besides hotels, a number of families built motels, especially during the 1940s to 1960s. Lately families have been turning their homes into bed and breakfast facilities. It seemed that as cars became more popular as a means of transportation, visitors would travel to the St. Margaret's Bay area, to spend a weekend or a few weeks vacationing around the Bay. Even today, families drive to Queensland Beach for an afternoon of swimming and relaxation in the sun. During the summer months, all you can see along the sandy beach are people lounging on their blankets or playing in the ocean with their cars filling the parking lot.

There are now new tourist attractions being developed around St. Margaret's Bay. Over the years various artists have been attracted to Peggy's Cove and Indian Harbour. In 1994, an art gallery was built in Peggy's Cove in honour of a well-known marine artist named William DeGarthe. Mr. DeGarthe was born in 1907 in Kaslo, Finland. At the age of nineteen he decided to see the world, but once he had visited Nova Scotia he remained here until his death in 1983. He tried several different types of employment but his first love was painting. It was not until he was encouraged by a fellow artist to quit his job, that he earnestly began to pursue a career as an artist on a full-time basis.

William DeGarthe fell in love with Peggy's Cove and decided to purchase a cottage there in 1948. At this time, he and his wife, the former Agnes Payne, were residing in Timberlea and were operating a commercial art and direct mailing service shop in Halifax. By 1963, they had moved to Peggy's Cove to live as residents of the small community. He opened a small art studio and began to sell his paintings for $35.00 each. After a few years he also decided to go to Italy to study how to create sculpture with marble, at the very same shop where Michaelangelo had studied 350 years before.

The subject of DeGarthe's marine paintings mainly consists of the fishermen of Peggy's Cove as they perform their tasks, on land and in their boats. He also produced sculptures in bronze, marble, alabaster, Florida sandstone and hydrocarl (white cement). His paintings and sculptures can be found in homes, offices and galleries on six continents.

During the late 1970s, William DeGarthe decided to begin a project which he predicted would take him at least ten years to

FISHERMEN'S MONUMENT CARVED BY WILLIAM DEGARTHE (1977-1983) IN PEGGY'S COVE. 1995

A. Withrow

DeGarthe's Gallery in Peggy's Cove, 1995

A. Withrow

complete. In his backyard there is a 100-foot piece of a Devonian outcropping. He began to carve a monument which he wanted to dedicate to the Canadian fishermen whom he strongly admired. The monument consists of 32 fishermen, wives, children, a guardian angel and a likeness of his pet seagull "Joe" in flight and of course "Peggy" as he envisioned her.

It is through the numerous paintings and sculptures of "Peggy" that the folklore of this mysterious fisherwoman has continued to develop. The story that has been passed down states that she was the sole survivor of a shipwreck off the rocks near Peggy's Cove. Peggy was supposed to be meeting her fiancé in Halifax, but she stayed in the area and married a local boy. It was DeGarthe who gave her life and a lasting place in Nova Scotia history.

The DeGarthes decided to leave the monument (and many of his remaining artworks) in the care of the provincial government. The province established the DeGarthe Gallery in his memory and tourists come from near and far to view his work, now housed in his former house and adjoining building.

CHAPTER SEVEN
Farming

The coastline of Nova Scotia consists of large granite rocks which makes it very difficult to farm the land. Nevertheless, there were a few farms located around St. Margaret's Bay. In 1839, a well-known newspaper editor, Joseph Howe, made the following observation in his newspaper, the *Novascotian*:

> At several of the settlements along the line of coast stretching between Halifax and the Bay, the people have no other resources but the fishery, for there is so little soil scattered over the granite rock upon which they reside, that sufficient is scarcely found in some places to make a cabbage garden ... there is abundance of soil, provided always that granite rocks are removed ...

DAUPHINEE FAMILY HAYING ON COLLISHAW'S FARM IN SEABRIGHT. C. 1900

PANS

The editorial goes on to mention that many men would find it very difficult to remove these rocks for farming and stated that it was almost impossible. He gives the men of St. Margaret's Bay credit for having the stamina to be able to overcome the hardships and to remove enough rocks to till the soil for planting. Some pictures, taken long ago, show families in their gardens planting potatoes or cutting hay. When we travel around the Bay and view the huge granite boulders it is difficult to imagine that hay was once growing in such places as Peggy's Cove.

Many of the farmers had animals such as horses and oxen to help with the farming. They also planted small gardens which helped to supply the family and neighbours with fresh vegetables and fruit. Hens and chickens were often kept to provide the family with fresh eggs and poultry.

Sheep were important to the farmers, mainly for the wool needed to make warm clothing for the family. The animals were

FAMILY RAKING HAY IN PEGGY'S COVE. C. 1910

PANS

GARRISON FAMILY PLANTING POTATOES AT INDIAN POINT IN GLEN HAVEN. C. 1910

PANS

PLANTING POTATOES IN TANTALLON. c. 1910

PANS

SHEARING SHEEP IN BOUTILIER'S POINT. LEFT TO RIGHT: SANDY BOUTILIER, DOUGLAS BOUTILIER AND NELLIE (BOUTILIER) CHRISTIE. c. 1930

Gary Meade

often kept on islands located in the Bay so that they could graze on the grass. Unfortunately the sheep could easily be stolen and often were found to disappear overnight. Women were often responsible for shearing the sheep. They would wash the wool and take the fleece to Chester to have it carded, so it would be ready for spinning. The wool would be used to make such items as mittens, stockings, sweaters, blankets and different types of underclothing.

The men would provide meat for the family by hunting in the woods around the St. Margaret's Bay. The woods were once plentiful with deer, rabbits, raccoons, foxes, bears and especially moose. It was quite a challenge for the hunters to enter the woods

HUNTING MOOSE IN ST. MARGARET'S BAY, TAKEN BY AMERICAN TOURISTS. (GARFIELD AND HARRY DAUPHINEE) 1925

Gary Meade

and come home with enough meat to supply their family for the winter. Hunting moose was also a sportsman's event, with men enjoying the challenge of shooting the largest animal they could find. This particular activity is not as popular as it once was since now only those who are lucky enough to receive a license to shoot moose are able to hunt this animal which is slowly disappearing.

CHAPTER EIGHT
Special Buildings

As the population in the communities around the Bay grew, so did the intricacy of its structured environment. The emergence of social and institutional buildings clearly indicates that the small villages were no longer only a group of houses but rather living communities.

The first retail establishment was the local general store which was found in each community regardless of its size. It provided more than just consumer goods. Because people usually went into the store on a regular basis, it developed into a social place. People went there to meet their neighbours to chat and gossip about such things as the political affairs of the times.

In 1894, Oswald Dauphinee of Hackett's Cove, purchased several lots of land for a total of $300.00. On one piece of property located near Boutilier's Cove, he erected a building which was to be used as his family home with a general store located downstairs. Many travellers would stop in, since they would have to pass directly in front of the building which is located on the main highway. There were also a number of sheds behind the store for the storage of supplies such as molasses, sugar, spices, hardware, and many other goods which would be brought by ships from Halifax to be sold at the store. For many years the building was known as the "Cork and Pickle Restaurant".

Across the road from the restaurant is a small pond which residents of the area call the "lily pond". Oswald Dauphinee travelled to Halifax frequently for supplies and one day he met an American who was staying at the same hotel on the Bay Road. The American had some lily roots. Mr. Dauphinee convinced the American to sell him one of the roots, which he carried home very carefully. When he arrived home, he placed the lily root in

OSWALD DAUPHINEE'S GENERAL STORE IN HACKETT'S COVE WITH LILY POND IN FOREGROUND. C. 1890

Gary Meade

a potato sack along with stone for weight and dropped the root into the pond. Only one lily pad appeared the first year, but over the years the number of lilies has grown.

These ponds as well as the ocean waters were also put to good use as a means of providing ice for the preservation of food. Years ago it was considered a necessary task to cut and store ice during the winter months to preserve food for the rest of the year. Several stores had icehouses built to house the blocks of ice that were cut out with a large saw, usually a cross-cut saw with one handle removed. The blocks of ice were cut from the Bay, lakes or ponds and then loaded on sleds drawn by horses and taken to the icehouse where the ice would be packed in sawdust. The sawdust would help to keep the ice frozen for longer periods of time. When the ice was needed it was easily removed from the building and if it was required for making ice cream, a block of ice was placed in a burlap bag. With the broadside of an ax or a

heavy hammer, it was broken into small pieces which could fit into the ice cream bucket.

Since the mid-1800s postal service has been available in the Bay area with the mail initially being distributed from one of the resident's homes or from the general store. Each community had its own postmaster who would hold the position for many years. Often the job would be passed on to another family member.

At first the letters and parcels were brought by horse and buggy from Halifax. Once the railroad was constructed in the area, the postman would pick up the mail at the railway station and deliver it to the designated distribution facilities. It has only been since the 1960s that modern post offices have been constructed in several communities around St. Margaret's Bay. They provide the residents with a place for private mail boxes and with the convenience of mailing parcels and buying stamps. The residents of the Bay still have their mail delivered to a mailbox by the postman or postwoman who now drives a car or truck rather than the horse and buggy of years ago. This has taken away the pleasure of the social aspect of picking up the mail at the local general store or the postmaster's home.

There have been many residents in the different communities who have been responsible for the task of delivering the mail. However, there is one gentlemen who should be mentioned for being responsible for mail delivery for more than a half a century. Charles Mahar of Glen Margaret travelled well over a million miles during his time as the local postman. For a number of years, Mr. Mahar would travel twice a day, through all kinds of weather, the twenty miles from the French Village Railway

Station to Glen Margaret, delivering parcels and letters and then back to the station a second time to pick up the newspapers.

Charles Mahar was the grandson of Thomas Mahar, who came from Ireland and settled in Glen Margaret. Charlie was born there in 1873, and started to deliver the mail when he was 18 years old. In the beginning he would pick up the mail at the crossroads from the stagecoach which ran between Halifax and Mahone Bay. Then in 1905 after the train station was built, he delivered mail in his small single seated wagon. Eventually cars became popular and Charlie purchased a station wagon to carry the mail.

In a newspaper article written in 1942, Charlie explains that a mail carrier's job often included other tasks besides mail delivery. None of his extra duties were expected of him, but he did not mind helping his neighbours by taking an important message for them to a family member residing in another village. A fisherman may have wanted information on the market value of fish, or he may have been requested to deliver a fresh baked pie

FRENCH VILLAGE RAILROAD STATION WITH CHARLIE MAHAR WAITING FOR THE MAIL TO ARRIVE. C. 1915

PANS

to someone's sick friend. It is sad this type of service has disappeared due to modern technology with post offices shifting from the local general store to government buildings, franchised outlets and "super boxes".

The small village of Peggy's Cove is the only community in Canada from which a person can mail a letter or postcard from a post office that was established in a lighthouse. During the summer months tourists can visit the Peggy's Cove lighthouse and send mail postmarked from this popular tourist village.

The most photographed landmark in this community is the tall, white lighthouse which stands overlooking the entrance to St. Margaret's Bay. Originally there was another lighthouse constructed in 1868 which was also used as the lighthouse keeper's residence. This building had a lantern on the roof to prevent ships from crashing upon the rocks. After the present lighthouse was built in 1914, the old building was used as a radio station for the Royal Canadian Navy. It was also used as a private residence until it was badly damaged during a storm and had to be demolished during the mid-1950s.

The present lighthouse stands 37 feet high and is built of concrete with reinforced iron. It is ten feet across at the base and six feet wide at the top. In 1934, it was equipped with a vapor light that had a screen, punctuated with opaque sections which revolved about the light to achieve the correct flashing effect. Eventually the light was changed to an oil light, but it still required the services of a lighthouse keeper. Finally when electricity came to the St. Margaret's Bay area an electric bulb was installed in the lighthouse. Since 1956, a 1000 watt bulb now helps the lighthouse to operate automatically without the services of a keeper.

As early as 1898, a survey team was sent to the Bay area to see if there was any possibility of a railway running through some of the communities surrounding the Bay. A decision was made that even though there may be many difficulties to overcome that a route would be quite practical and that construction of the line should begin as soon as possible.

Several railway stations were built along the line with only one of the structures still standing today. The French Village Railway Station was erected at the Crossroads at the turn of the century, while the area was still part of the original French Village community. This station was instrumental in receiving the mail

PEGGY'S COVE SHOWING BOTH THE OLD AND NEW LIGHTHOUSES. C. 1920

PANS

HUBBARDS RAILWAY STATION. C. 1955

PANS

as well as visitors to the Head of St. Margaret's Bay area for many years. This building was built along the "shingled style" which was a popular design with the railroad, since the majority of stations were constructed along the same architectural lines.

A second station was constructed at Ingramport in 1905, because this small community, at the turn of the century, was a very active lumbering town. Once the community was no longer involved in the lumbering trade, the need for the station slowly came to an end. It was not until 1960 that the decision was finally made to demolish the structure.

A third railway depot was erected in Hubbards. The popularity of this small resort made the railway important for the arrival of visitors during their summer vacations. This station also disappeared when it was demolished during the 1960s. Of the three buildings, only the French Village Railway Station is still standing. It is now privately owned and used as a craft store for tourists who now drive around the Bay in their automobiles rather than taking the train.

Unfortunately, during the last few decades, the railway has been in a decline. As a means for travelling and delivering mail it is no longer required, mainly due to the more modern means of transportation. Railroad tracks around the Bay have been removed and are now used as recreational trails.

Volunteer fire departments were organized in the Bay area around 1949 when the County of Halifax bought a fire truck and placed it in Black Point. The necessity of having an organization available to fight fires was obvious as you look back and see how many homes, businesses and outbuildings were lost due to fires. Several meetings had been held in the village to form a volunteer fire department. During this period of organization the fire truck had been kept in a garage or barn until a building could be found to be used as a fire station. When a fire broke out the residents of the communities would hope that someone who could drive the truck would be available.

By 1952, several meetings had taken place in Hubbards, Black Point, Boutilier's Point and Head of St. Margaret's Bay. Through the efforts of Granville Snair, who was the county councillor at this time, and other Bay residents, steps were taken to find a place to keep the fire truck. Until 1955, it had been kept in several different places including the basement of Romkey's, now the Bizee Centre, where Harold Whittier was responsible for maintaining the truck. In 1956, the fire department purchased from the County for $19.00, an old two-room schoolhouse which had been built in 1907, and moved it from Boutilier's Point to Black Point.

THE NEW DISTRICT NO. 1 FIRE STATION AND HALL IN BLACK POINT. 1995

A. Withrow

A few years ago, a larger, modern facility was constructed and several more full-time firemen were hired to fight the fires. This year the Black Point Fire Department is planning to celebrate its fortieth anniversary.

The telephone plays an important role in informing the people of the different communities that a fire has broken out in someone's home. It was in 1898 that poles were placed along the South Shore so people would be able to communicate with one another through this new invention. Men from the Bay area were hired to dig the holes and to place the poles along the highway, so it meant they had to travel for a few weeks through the different communities around the province. In those days they would travel in a covered wagon which was used to sleep in and to carry supplies. The men would sometimes sleep in someone's backyard, out under the stars, and often met interesting people.

Telephone operators were hired and the telephone lines were set up in their homes so the phones could be monitored 24 hours a day. In the beginning St. Margaret's Bay had two operators, one in Hubbards and the other in Head of St. Margaret's Bay. The operators knew where everyone lived and would alert the fire departments of any emergencies that arose within the communities. Three long rings would make everyone in the area aware that something had happening and by lifting the receiver residents were able to find out for themselves where the fire was. Later a siren was placed on the roof of the fire station. During the 1980s, a paging system was installed which simpli-

fied matters for the volunteers. By this time several other volunteer fire departments were organized in several other communities around the Bay such as Head of St. Margaret's Bay, Seabright and Hubbards.

Another modern convenience to be brought to St. Margaret's Bay was the hydro station which was constructed during the early 1920s. The actual work began in May 1920, and continued for four years at Head of St. Margaret's Bay.

The high power rates being paid in the city brought about the need for a cheaper source of electricity. The cost of building a power development of sufficient magnitude to cover the new demand made it necessary to have the help of the Nova Scotia government. Recommendations were made to the province for the development of two sites at St. Margaret's Bay. The Tidewater Generating plant on the shores of the Bay along with another plant located on the Northeast River would provide the city with 20 million kilowatts of power a year.

Members of the general public were fearful of what it would mean to have the power plant so close to their homes and it made them hesitant. Farmers in the Bay expressed concerns that electricity would leak into the ground, affecting their livestock and the vegetation.

From the beginning discussions were held between the N.S. Power Commission and the City of Halifax to negotiate the contract plans for utilizing the power from the Bay. In a report published in a Halifax newspaper, the *Evening Mail*, to the residents of Halifax, it discussed how the plant was well designed. It also stated the it was constructed along modern lines and should provide a reliable power service for the city. Nevertheless, its construction altered the landscape by diverting a river and drying up a lake to create more land.

Another problem involved the ownership of the system. Many people felt that the plant should not be owned by a private corporation because power rates would not be regulated. Several possibilities were discussed until the decision was made in February 1922 for the Nova Scotian Tramways and Power Commission to organize operations for power service. The line from St. Margaret's Bay to Halifax was the first large scale operation to be undertaken by the commission and was a model for the installation of future hydro plants throughout the province.

CHAPTER NINE
Organizations, Associations and Clubs

In 1860 the men of St. Margaret's Bay decided to erect a union hall in French Village. Land was provided from Ersom Boutilier who received four shares for the property. A large building was constructed and it was not long before meetings were being held in the new Union Hall of St. Margaret's Bay. The members began by organizing their association's rules and regulations regarding those who wished to have shares in the organization. The number of shares a member received depended upon the number of pounds they wished to pay. One pound purchased one share.

Other rules that were enforced concerned a member's conduct. For example, those who came to a meeting intoxicated were fined and if they caused a disturbance they would be turned out and not allowed back in until they were sober. The organization also made decisions regarding the hourly wage that was to be paid for a day's labour.

UNION HALL ONCE LOCATED IN FRENCH VILLAGE. C. 1915

PANS

A LODGE GROUP PICTURE TAKEN ON THE VERANDAH OF THE ICE CREAM PARLOUR IN SEABRIGHT. C. 1930

PANS

Other groups were also organized in the Bay such as the Grand Lodge of British Templars, International Order of Good Templars, Independent Order of Odd Fellows Manchester Unity and the Orangemen. The International Order of Good Templars was instituted on February 5, 1867. This organization required its members to abstain from the consumption of alcoholic beverages. This group saw that there were more negative aspects to alcohol than there were positive benefits. They felt that it was the cause of unhappiness and degeneracy in society. As a result the members formed a variety of temperance organizations which were largely religious and rural in nature.

The Orangemen was an association of Protestants who swore they would support King William III of the House of Orange, when he succeeded to the throne of England. It was customary to hold an annual celebration to mark the victory of William III over James II, a catholic, at the Battle of Boyne in July 1690. The association became known around 1795 when the Orange Society was formed in Ulster, Ireland. When the Irish settlers emigrated to Nova Scotia, an influx of Irishmen settled in the Bay and organized their own society in 1849. They built meeting halls in several communities. Around 1900, Peggy's Cove residents erected the Orange Lodge and used it as a Lodge Hall for a number of years. Eventually the hall was used by the community for their dances and church socials, after it was rebuilt and enlarged in 1950. In nearby Indian Harbour, another Orangeman's Hall that was built in 1911 still stands on the main highway. The Italianate styled building was owned by the

Anglican Diocese and called the St. Andrew's Anglican Church Hall, until it was recently purchased by a glass company.

The Oddfellow's Lodge was founded in the Seabright area on February 15, 1901, by Nathan Hubley. When it was first formed the members would meet in the old Union Hall in French Village, then in the upper floor of Nathan Hubley's old store. This store eventually became the Oddfellow's Hall until it was demolished and replaced by the present structure. The new hall was erected in 1976 on the same site but set a little further back from the highway.

In Hubbards the Independent Order of Odd Fellows Manchester Unity was formed at the turn of the century. They built a structure in which to hold their meetings and it was referred to as the Manchester Hall. This popular hall provided a place for entertainment when travelling acts would come to the area. Also entertainment was often provided by members of the community who probably began acting out plays in parlors as games. Dressing in costumes was not restricted to any particular time of the year, but was done as a means of raising money for the different organizations. After 1925, when electricity was supplied to the community, movies were shown there and the building was known as the Hubb Theatre. This structure was eventually demolished in 1970.

The largest building located in Seabright is the St. Margaret's Bay Branch 116 of the Royal Canadian Legion. This association continues to represent the tireless fund-raising efforts of many of the residents in and around the Seabright community. When the legion members began their organization, meetings were first held in Glen Margaret until fire destroyed the hall in 1947. They moved the meetings to the Victoria School in Glen Haven, but a few years later they made the decision to purchase land in Seabright to build their own hall.

It was not until 1964 that the building was constructed and then expanded ten years later. When the land was first purchased on November 4, 1951, the Legion members dedicated a War Memorial on the site. The memorial was erected to remind the residents of those men who lost their lives fighting for the war effort. There were a number of young men from the local region who did not come home again after serving their country during the First and Second World Wars.

DURING WORLD WAR II A PLANE LANDED DUE TO ENGINE TROUBLE, ON SNAKE LAKE IN INGRAMPORT; A ROAD WAS MADE TO TOW THE PLANE OUT. C. 1941

PANS

During the time that the Legion was being organized in Seabright, the Masonic Lodge was underway in Head of St. Margaret's Bay. On December 13, 1950, a meeting was held by the Masonic Brethren in the St. James Church Hall in Boutilier's Point. There were twenty-three members present from twelve lodges. The new lodge would be called the St. Margaret's Lodge. Meetings were held on the first Thursday of every month in Head of St. Margaret's Bay. Once the lodge had been formed, the members planned to have their own premises constructed. In 1953, Brother Allen donated the land beside the Baptist Church located on the St. Margaret's Bay Road. The group established their goals from the beginning and have continued to grow. The hall is still standing and is often used for different social functions which are often held in the community.

Numerous other associations and organizations have played a role in supplying the St. Margaret's Bay residents with a chance to get together for one reason or another. During the late 1930s, the Chronicle Company Limited had purchased a house, formerly built by James Mason around 1820, located on the Mason Point Road. The owner of this company provided a number of unfortunate children with the opportunity to spend some time at this country place which was given the name of Camp Sunshine.

In 1953, the Camp was sold to the Anglican Diocese who also operate a summer camp for children of the Anglican faith and it was renamed the Anglican Youth Camp. Many children from the Bay area and from the City of Halifax, have enjoyed a week or two learning new activities, swimming, making crafts and playing sports. They also made long-lasting friendships with others who came to summer camp each year while this facility was in operation. Today the buildings have been demolished and the Anglican Youth Camp is gone, replaced by a modern home owned by David and Margaret Fountain.

The Girl Guides of Canada have been organized in the area since the early 1900s. Several different group districts have been formed in St. Margaret's Bay over the years. Women have played a part in teaching the young girls of the Bay how to survive in the outdoors, techniques in cooking, how to knit, sew, and to have fun. Each summer the girls and their leaders go to camp for a weekend and are taught the different ways one goes about cooking and sleeping in the great outdoors. Even during the 1930s the Girl Guides spent a period of time earning their badges by doing the various tasks expected by their leaders. Today the

GIRL GUIDE LEADERS AT A GUIDE CAMP: MS. GATES; O. FERGUSON; K. ROMANS, M. ROBERTS; V. DOREY; A. BULTILT; MS. PUBLICOVER; MRS. SCHENK; M. MAHAR; V. MORGAN. C. 1933

PANS

Organizations, Associations and Clubs **79**

group is still visible in the Bay, however their summer excursions are now conducted at a Girl Guide camp in another part of the province.

Besides these types of associations and groups there were other organizations that were formed which involved both amateur and competitive sports. For many years ice skating was a favourite pastime for the children of the St. Margaret's Bay area. There were numerous lakes and coves that were perfect for ice skating and playing hockey once they were frozen. There were several hockey teams formed in the Bay area. For example, in 1939 there was the Tantallon Canadians and later during the 1950s fans cheered the Hubbards Tuna. Not all hockey games were organized and played in a rink. Many of the young people of the Bay would spend their winter afternoons enjoying a friendly game of hockey on the nearest patch of ice.

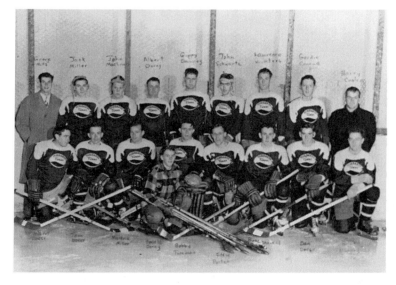

HUBBARDS COVE HOCKEY TEAM CALLED HUBBARDS TUNA (SEE APPENDIX). C. 1950

PANS

PLAYING HOCKEY ON FROST FISH COVE IN CONNOLLY'S POINT, GLEN HAVEN. C. 1918

PANS

Today in the Bay area, hockey, soccer and baseball are well organized activities which involve children and adults of all ages. Sailing is as popular as ever, and has become accessible to more people with the opening of St. Margaret's Bay Sailing Club's new facilities at Mariners' Anchorage in French Village.

New organizations and societies have been organized during the last few years to preserve the history of St. Margaret's Bay. In 1985, a Bicentennial Committee was formed under the direction of Gary Meade of Head of St. Margaret's Bay. Several events were organized to celebrate the 200th anniversary of the settlement of the St. Margaret's Bay area. The St. Margaret's Bay

heritage society erected a cairn to commemorate this historical event. The cairn is made from small beach stones and is located on the parking lot for Black Point Beach. Stated on the bronze plaque is the following: "This cairn is dedicated to the early settlers of St. Margaret's Bay who were persuaded by Gov. John Parr to settle here in the 1780s". Unfortunately the society eventually disbanded. Another heritage society has now been formed in Hubbards which promotes the preservation of the history of this small community.

CHAPTER TEN
Rum-running

Prohibition played a significant role in Nova Scotia's history. Rum-running seemed to escalate when the United States implemented the 18th Amendment in January 1920. Nova Scotia fishermen and ship owners, along with the fishermen in the States and other Maritime provinces, organized a smuggling system which fooled many government officials and members of the police forces. Liquor was hidden in large quantities in the woods, barns, sheds, lakes, wharves and other secret hiding places.

Many tales can be told by oldtimers concerning the rum-runners who risked their lives trying to make a fast buck. The men who were unemployed saw rum-running as an alternative to no work at all and not knowing where their next meal would come from. Also, the difference in pay between an honest job as a fisherman or a lumberman and liquor smuggling, made the decision to risk everything an easy one to make.

The system that was set up for smuggling the goods was very complex. Ships would sail for 'rum row' as it was commonly called, to pass over their stock of liquor to the American boats that would sneak past the coast guards to the waiting ships. 'Rum row' was the name given to the twelve mile limit beyond the Eastern United States. American customs officials had no jurisdiction outside this limit. The tricky part involved sneaking back to shore.

Runs were also being made off the Nova Scotia coastline, however the contact ships had to stay only three miles from shore. Therefore, it was easier to transport the liquor and there was less risk of being caught. The contacts usually had small motor boats that could outrun the customs officers. The rum-runners would have designated hiding places to stash the goods until they could pass the liquor on to the bootleggers.

Nova Scotia was an excellent haven for rum-running operations since the coastline has hundreds of coves, inlets, and islands which provided ideal hiding spots. The bootleggers also had to hide their supplies in case of police raids on their establishments. There were often bogus hiding places in such places as the woods, fireplaces, stairwells, under counters, between floorboards and secret rooms.

Ships also had areas sectioned off to conceal the liquor from the officials. One ship had its entire keel constructed with a double lining. Another ship had a space beneath the engines which was capable of holding more than 1000 cases of liquor. Other methods of concealment involved covering the cases with a load of freshly caught fish. When a ship had a full cargo of liquor it was known by those involved in the trade. The ships usually had a white line painted along their hulls and when full the ship would be low in the water with the paint mark situated below the water line.

St. Margaret's Bay was ideal for smuggling. Since the illegal activities of rum-running took place not that long ago, people who had family members involved are still hesitant to talk about it. Some residents will speak about the rum-runners if names are not recorded. It is known that rum-running did occur here in the Bay and that some residents were prosecuted by the law.

There are stories that have been told regarding illegal activities involving people in the Bay area. For example, one moonlit night some villagers were on their way home from a dance when they noticed a couple of strange cars near a canteen. As they watched they observed that one of the cars which was facing the water kept turning its lights on and off. They were apparently signalling boats that were anchored off the shore. As they continued to watch, the boats began to come ashore and unloaded some kegs which were quickly transported away in the cars.

Another incident involved a big ship anchored near Shut In Island. With a telescope a person could see the men walking on the deck of the ship. Later it was discovered that a cutter had chased the boat into the bay and they had hidden behind the island. It was obvious that the boat was well stocked with liquor because it was low in the water.

The area around Tantallon was said to be the place where most of the rum-running activities took place during this time period. Stories have been told of people being shot trying to steal someone's cache or being beaten with a set of brass knuckles for stealing from a rum-runner. Often neighbours who did not agree with these illegal activities, would take matters into their own hands. Rather than squeal to the police and risk retaliation, they altered the taste of the liquor by adding such things as kerosene as one mother was said to have done.

Years later after prohibition ended, kegs of liquor and rum bottles were known to have been found well preserved. In Tantallon three kegs of liquor and several rum bottles were apparently found by someone digging in a sawdust pile prior to doing some construction work.

During the 1930s the Nova Scotia Liquor Commission was organized and given complete control over liquor sales in Nova Scotia. The government decided the time involved in trying to catch the rum-runners could be eliminated if controls were put into effect concerning the selling of liquor. It also provided a great deal of revenue for the Nova Scotia government.

TAKEN FRON SMITH PROPERTY ON WHYNACHT'S POINT IN TANTALLON. C. 1915

PANS

NEHEMIAH DOREY WITH FAMILY IN FRONT OF HOME IN TANTALLON. C. 1915

PANS

CHAPTER ELEVEN
Houses in the Bay

In the St. Margaret's Bay area, there are approximately 375 houses (erected prior to 1914) that are still standing. The majority of them were built in the vernacular style, which was basically the style preferred by the fishermen or farmers. Often they would add dormers to the roofs, a style brought to Nova Scotia by the Scottish settlers. The architectural term most people commonly use to describe this type of structure is the Cape Cod style. By looking at old pictures we can see that some structures have changed over the years. Additional rooms and ornamentation were often added and the shape of the roof changed. The most obvious change that has taken place is the landscape around the properties. Trees have either disappeared now or, conversely, been replanted, hiding the buildings from our view as we travel around the Bay.

Still standing in Glen Margaret is the home of John Fraser Junior which was built by John Lambert. Mr. Lambert was responsible for the construction of several houses situated in the community. This particular home was built around 1842, when John Fraser's father gave him the land as a wedding present when he married Hannah Moser, the daughter of John Moser.

The Fraser family were Loyalists who first settled in Shelburne, Nova Scotia when the influx of immigrants moved here from the United States during the early 1780s. Apparently, the story that has been passed down through the family states that John Fraser, as a young lad, was a stowaway on one of John Boutilier's ships, when it docked one day in Shelburne. The Boutilier family allowed him to stay. They took him in and brought him up as one of their own. John Fraser married Susan Boutilier and settled in Glen Margaret.

FRED FRASER'S HOME BUILT C. 1842 IN GLEN MARGARET. C. 1925

PANS

ISAAC DAUPHINEE WITH FAMILY IN FRONT OF HOME IN TANTALLON. C. 1900

PANS

In 1801, John Fraser purchased land from James Creighton and as the Fraser family grew, several homes were erected in the Glen Margaret area. The house that had been built for John Fraser Junior has a black band painted around the top of the chimney. This particular sign was used to indicate to others that the home was owned by a Loyalist family.

A number of homes in the Tantallon area that were constructed by the Dauphinee family are also still standing. Unfortunately one home in particular which was built by Isaac Dauphinee has disappeared. In a picture of the house taken around 1925, we can see that the facade of the home shows two Scottish dormers located on the roof. The entrance was an enclosed small front porch which was not an unusual feature for this time period. Added to the left side of the building is an extension which was often built as a summer kitchen. Most homes added this addition either to the side or back portion of the structures. This helped to prevent the heat from the wood stove from entering the rest of the home while the women were busy cooking the family meals during the hot summer months.

Another family to settle in the Tantallon community were the Swallows. James Swallow purchased a piece of property from

SWALLOW FAMILY IN FRONT OF HOMESTEAD IN TANTALLON. C. 1890

PANS

John R. Harshman (Hurshman) in 1871 to build his homestead at the Head of the Bay not far from the railway station. The family resided in this house for more than one hunderd years. Today this Greek Revival styled home has a verandah across the facade. The trees that once stood around it have long disappeared. The summer kitchen has been removed and the windows and chimney have been changed.

Around the mid-1800s, Peter George Boutilier, a fisherman, built a large two-and-one-half storey home in French

Village. This particular house was designed in the New England style and has changed very little during the last 150 years since its construction. The Boutilier family settled in this small community during the 1780s after moving from the Lunenburg area and have owned this property since it was constructed.

In 1869, Joseph Shankel settled with his family in Hubbard's Cove after he moved from Greenfield, Nova Scotia. He purchased land and built his home near the river so that he could erect a mill in back of his property. Mr. Shankel's home is described as being constructed in the "picturesque style", mainly because of the gingerbread bargeboard trim located along the eaves of the roof.

The home was also known to have been used as a way station with stables in back to house the horses. When cars became popular, gas pumps were added and the stables were removed. When the road was paved the home was moved back from the road and the pumps disappeared. Near the family home, several of Mr. Shankel's sons built their homes which are still standing today. Joseph Shankel Junior erected two homes next door to his parent's residence and two

SCENE SHOWING SADDLER'S HOMESTEAD NEAR WOODEN'S RIVER IN SEABRIGHT. C. 1910

PANS

more sons, Stewart and Malachi Shankel constructed their houses near the St. Luke's Anglican Church. The houses were built during the late 1870s and the early 1880s, either in the Greek Revival style or the Modified Gothic style. Three of the houses have not changed their architectural design. Malachi Shankel's former home has had additions made to it and is now known as the Anchorage Motel and Cabins. It is located on the site of the first Hubbards schoolhouse.

CHAPTER TWELVE
The Automobile

At the turn of the 20th century a number of new inventions were being developed. The invention of the automobile changed the way we would travel, at first for short jaunts and eventually for longer trips. The automobile was a novelty in the beginning with only those who could afford to buy them, seen driving around the communities. As time progressed the car became a necessity, as a means of getting to work and as an emergency vehicle.

One of the first families to purchase a vehicle in the St. Margaret's Bay area was Oswald Dauphinee of Hackett's Cove. His car was large enough for the family to sit in and enjoy a sunny afternoon drive around the Bay. As time passed the automobile became less expensive for the times and then became a common sight.

In order to promote the automobile, motor tours were organized by the companies who first produced them. In 1904, Archie Pelton of Berwick, Nova Scotia and a Mr. Porter of Kentville, Nova Scotia went together to the first automobile show which was held in New York City. While they were there they purchased two Curved Dash Oldsmobiles and had them shipped back home. These were the first two cars in the province for resale. Pelton dismantled the cars to study how they were built and then put them back together again. He took them to Halifax and sold them; this was the beginning of the first car dealership in Nova Scotia.

Two brothers by the name of McKay decided in 1910 to seriously consider manufacturing the automobile here in Nova Scotia. At this time, a coupe sold for $1,450.00 with a larger model costing $2,050.00. The McKay Car Company produced

MCKAY MOTOR TOUR STOPPING IN HUBBARDS FOR A REST. 1913

two models, one a 30 h.p. Torpedo Coupe and the other a 40 h.p. five passenger touring car.

In 1913, the *Halifax Herald* newspaper sponsored a race from Halifax to Yarmouth, which included 210 miles via the Annapolis Valley and back by way of the South Shore, another 215 miles. This race was opened to all cars and was won by a McKay car, driven by Mr. Beacraft. Pictures were taken of the event when the group stopped at Hubbards Cove for refreshments and a short rest.

As the years passed more and more cars were being driven by some of the families residing in the Bay. Oswald Dauphinee and his family were often seen in Hackett's Cove driving around in his Baby Grand Chev. Byron Dauphinee was one of the first residents to purchase the popular Model T. Several years later cars were seen around the Bay being driven by Pat Isnor in 1925 and by 1942, Charlie Barnes of Head of St. Margaret's Bay. Not long after the automobile was invented, another motorized invention was being driven in the Bay area and because it was

DAUPHINEE FAMILY CAR IN TANTALLON. C. 1925

PANS

PAT ISNOR IN HIS CAR IN GLEN MARGARET. C. 1925

PANS

CHARLIE BARNES' CAR IN HEAD OF ST. MARGARET'S BAY. C. 1942

PANS

MRS. HANNAH VAUGHAN, 86 YEARS OLD, ENJOYING A MOTORCYCLE RIDE IN HACKETT'S COVE. 1928

PANS

similar in style to a bicycle, it was called the motorcycle. This invention had an attachment on the side to carry a passenger. Around 1928, when Hannah Vaughan of Hackett's Cove was 86 years old, she was given the opportunity to have a ride in such a motor contraption.

CHAPTER THIRTEEN
New Businesses

Some of the old businesses that were once part of the St. Margaret's Bay communities have disappeared over the years. However new ones have continued to develop and have become successful as they provide employment for many of the residents living in the area. These new businesses have been a blessing to many because of the shortage of jobs that has become a growing concern for everyone. Many people now work in the City of Halifax, since it is now a short trip by car. But for those who wish to remain in their communities to work the NAUTEL plant, in Hackett's Cove, has made this decision a possibility.

Nautical Electronics Laboratories Limited (NAUTEL) is owned by the personnel within its own workforce. The president and major shareholder is Dennis Covill, who emigrated to Canada in 1955, from London, England. Mr. Covill decided that this type of industry could be located in the Hackett's Cove area mainly because of its proximity to the Atlantic Ocean. The type of products they develop are for oceanographic institutions.

NAUTEL PLANT IN HACKETT'S COVE 1995

A. Withrow

They offer a design and production service in such specialized fields as: solid state communication systems, transmitters and receivers, telemetry systems and components and navigation systems and components.

Over the years the business has continued to grow with the workforce steadily increasing. The original plant was built in the 1970s with a major expansion taking place in 1982 and once again during the early 1990s. The business also has an affiliate of NAUTEL called Polestar which is a small production facility in Bangor, Maine.

Family businesses continue to develop in the Bay, especially in the Black Point community. The Snair family started several businesses in the area beginning during the 1940s. Granville Snair first established a plumbing and electrical business in his

SNAIRS BAKERY TODAY IN BLACK POINT. 1995

A. Withrow

A MODERN STRIP MALL AT THE CROSSROADS IN TANTALLON. 1995

A. Withrow

home and by 1961 it had grown to such an extent he had to purchase premises in which to conduct his business. Also during the 1940s, Roy Snair opened a canteen where he served meals with freshly baked bread and rolls. This business has continued to expand today with the Snair Bakery providing bread, rolls and other baked goods to a number of grocery stores within the province.

It was not until the late 1970s that the people of St. Margaret's Bay were given the opportunity to purchase their groceries and other necessary items at a large shopping mall. In 1976, Lester Hubley, a businessman, decided to provide the residents of the Bay area with a large scaled commercial and residential development on 300 acres of land, located in the Upper Tantallon community. He was also instrumental in the St. Margaret's Bay Rink being constructed in the same area, thus providing a place for children and their parents to skate or play hockey without having to depend on the elements of winter. The outdoor pool which was added to the facility, has been very popular with summer swimmers. This commercial enterprise is still being developed today with several eating establishments and other professional services continuing to emerge in the area.

* * *

St. Margaret's Bay has seen many changes since the construction of Highway 103 made the urban centres quickly accessible. More and more summer cottages have been converted to year-round homes as owners realized that they could have the best of both worlds; some have even brought their businesses with them. New subdivisions are no longer a novelty. As the demand for consumer services and conveniences has increased, small local establishments have sometimes given way to large chain stores.

In 1996, the Halifax County section of St. Margaret's Bay (Peggy's Cove to Hubbards) became part of the Halifax Regional Municipality. Inevitably, additional changes will take place as a result of the merger, but it is unlikely that the character and appeal of the Bay will ever be diminished.

SLAUNWHITE FAMILY - JAMES SLAUWHITE WITH HIS SONS. C. 1905

PANS

MR. AND MRS. ARCH GATES STANDING ON THE SIDE OF THE ROAD IN FRONT OF UNION HALL IN FRENCH VILLAGE. C. 1910

PANS

CHAPTER FOURTEEN
Families

The following is a poll tax list taken in 1792/93, listing approximately 59 families* in the St. Margaret's Bay area: (annotated by Mr. T. Punch of Halifax, NS in 1988)

ADAMS, William - a farmer, 4 cattle, a Loyalist
ANDREWS, John - a farmer, 2 cows, a Foreign Protestant
BARRY, William
BOUTILIER, George - a farmer, 6 cattle, a Foreign Protestant
BOUTILIER, Jacques - a farmer, 6 cattle, a Foreign Protestant
BOUTILIER, James - master of trading vessel, 6 cows, a Foreign Protestant
BOUTILIER, James Frederick - a boatmaster, 8 cattle, a Foreign Protestant
BOUTILIER, John - a farmer, 6 cows, a Foreign Protestant
    (Born in Lunenburg, in 1759, brother of James Frederick Boutilier. He married Hanna
    Knickel in 1779 and had 12 children. He died at St. Margaret's Bay ca.1823/24.)
BOUTILIER, John - a Foreign Protestant
BOUTILIER, John George - a farmer, 3 cows, Foreign Protestant
    (Born in Lunenburg, in 1756, a brother of James and John Boutilier and died 1831 in St.
    Margaret's Bay, married in 1780 at Lunenburg to Catherine Elizabeth Leau (Lowe) and
    had 12 children.)
BULKELEY, J.F., Esquire - a farmer, Irish
CADEY, Robert - a farmer, 5 cattle
CALDWELL, Hugh - a farmer, 2 cattle
CARROL, Michael - Irish
CLOYNE, John - Hessian Veteran
CORNEY, Waldon - a farmer, 2 cows
COULEN, William - a labourer, Newfoundland Irish
CROUCHER, James - a farmer, 6 cattle & 20 sheep, Newfoundland Irish
CROUCHER, Samuel - Newfoundland Irish
    (Samuel and James were brothers, believed to be from Newfoundland. James received 500
    acres in July 1784 at St. Margaret's Bay and was married two or three times, had 11
    children. Samuel (1759-1794) married Eleanor Berry and had 2 children.)

DAUPHINEE, Christopher - a farmer, 6 cattle, Foreign Protestant

DAUPHINEE, John - a farmer, 3 cows, Foreign Protestant

> (Christopher, George and John Dauphinee were brothers and the sons of Jean Dauphinee and Marie-Elizabeth Banvard of Montbeliard. Christopher (1756-1841) married Sarah P. Veinot and had 11/12 children. George (1764-1811) married 1783 to Sarah Veinot and also had 11 children. John (1757-1835) received 650 acres at the Bay in 1785 and married 1776 at Lunenburg to Mary Elizabeth Boutilier and had 14 children.)

DAWSEY, Matthew - a labourer

FOLEY, Nicholas

FREDERICK, Adam - a farmer, 2 cows, Foreign Protestant

GRIFFITH, James - a labourer

HARNISH, Gutlip - a farmer, 10 cattle, Foreign Protestant

> (Gottlieb John Harnish (1737-1826) came from Saxony in 1751 and married in 1760 to Charlotte Mertz, at Lunenburg, had 9 children.)

HEMLOCK, James - a boatmaster, 8 cattle, Scottish

HEMLOCK, James - a boatmaster, Scottish

HEMLOCK, John, Jr. - a farmer, 10 cattle, 12 sheep, Scottish

HEMLOCK, William - a farmer, Scottish

> (John Hemlock or Umlah, Sr. was the father of the other three. He was Scots born and came to Nova Scotia in 1762 from Philadelphia. He died 1821 at Todd's Island, age 89. Married Isabella MacDonald, and had 10 children, including the three mentioned here. James born 1771 in Chester, married 1795 at Halifax, to Ann Mary MacDonald and had 6 children. The second James should be John Jr. (1758-1849) who married 1784 at Halifax to Mary Redmond and had 10 children. William (1770-1839/40) married in 1797 at Halifax to Anne Wagner and had 12 children.)

HORNSBY, John - a farmer, 3 cows

JANPARIEN, Christopher - Foreign Protestant

JOLLYMORE, George - boatmaster, 3 cattle, Foreign Protestant

JOLLYMORE, James - a farmer, 2 cows, Foreign Protestant

> (George and James Jollymore were brothers and sons of Pierre Jolimois from Montbeliard. George Frederick Jollymore (1763-1822) married Catherine Maillard and had 5 children. James, his brother (1754-1834) died at Chester, Nova Scotia, married at Lunenburg in 1777 to Catherine Robar, had 9 children. He was granted 500 acres on the west side of the Bay in 1792.)

JOUDRAY, James - a farmer, 20 sheep, Foreign Protestant

KELLY, Hugh - a farmer, 1 horse, 4 cows, Loyalist

LEWIS, Henry - a farmer

LORING, John - a labourer

McDONALD, Hugh - a farmer, 4 cattle, Loyalist

> (Hugh was the son of Jannett McDonald. He was a corporal and Loyalist who received 400 acres at the Bay in 1785, as did Alexander McDonald.)

McGuire, Patrick - a labourer

MARCHAND, George - 3 cattle

MARRIOTT, Peter - a farmer, 6 cattle, Foreign Protestant

(John Peter Marriott (1765-1838) was the son of Etienne Mariette of Montbeliard who came to Nova Scotia in 1752, married (1) in 1785 at Lunenburg to Mary Elizabeth Veinot and had 8 children. he married (2) to Anne Catherine Boutilier. He died at Harrietsfield, NS.)

MARRISHAL, Nicholas - a farmer, 2 cows

MINGO, John - Foreign Protestant

MOLLIER, George

MOLLIER, John

MONYGOMERY, William - a farmer, 1 cow

MOORE, William - a farmer

O'BRIEN, John - planter, Irish

PHELON, John - labourer, Irish

PHILKES, Barney - labourer

SLAUGHENWHITE, _____ - 5 cows, Foreign Protestant

(This would be John Jacob Slauenwhite of Lunenburg. His son John Frederick, born 1769, married in 1792 at Lunenburg to Elizabeth Weagle and had a large family. Name originally spelt SCHLAGENTWEIT and came from Wurttemburg, Germany in 1752.)

STUDARDS, James

TROOP, John - a farmer, 3 cattle

(When he received 500 acres on the west side of the Bay he had already been in Nova Scotia for 18 years. He married 1799 at Halifax to Rebecca Reffrew (1744-1813) the widow of John Herring, and had three sons, of which two, George and William Troop received part of the Peggy's Cove grant with Kayzer and Izenhaur on 10 June 1810.)

WAMBOULT, Adam - a farmer, 2 horses, 6 cattle, Foreign Protestant

(John Adam Wambold was born at Lunenburg in 1755, a son of Johann Adam Wambolt from Hesse-Darmstadt, Germany, and Maria Barbara Hawes (his second wife). He received 500 acres in two different locations on the Bay in 1786. He married at Lunenburg in 1783 to Mary Elizabeth Dauphinee and had several children.)

WAMBOULT, Christopher - boatmaster, Foreign Protestant

WESTAVER, Conrad - a farmer, 2 cows, Foreign Protestant

(John Conrad Westhaver, born in Lunenburg in 1758, a son of Johann Michael and Anna Christina Westhoffer who came to Nova Scotia from Palatinate, Germany in 1751. Conrad married in 1783 to Catherine Boutilier and had 11 children.)

WOODIN, William - a farmer, 4 cattle, Loyalist

*   *Names are spelled the way they had been recorded.*

WILLIAM AND HARRIET COVEY IN HACKETT'S COVE. C. 1910

PANS

JACK SMITH OF WHYNACHT'S POINT BEING TAPED BY FOLKLORIST HELEN CREIGHTON. C. 1950

PANS

CHAPTER FIFTEEN
Family Genealogies

The following is a partial genealogy of several families who still have descendants residing in the St. Margaret's Bay area:

BOUTILIER FAMILY: JAMES

James BOUTILIER b. 23 Nov. 1760 - 4th son of 13 children born to Jean George BOUTILIER and Catherine MAILLER. d. 1841 at the age of 81 in Sou'west Cove, buried in Boutilier's Cove, Hackett's Cove, beside his wife Susan Elizabeth MARRIETTE d. 1838, dau. of Peter MARRIETTE of French Village (Frost Fish Cove).

Children:
1) Anna Catherine b. 1781 m. John BOUTILIER (moved to Cape Breton)
2) John Peter b. 21 Nov. 1782 m. Mary BURGOYNE in 1809
3) John James b. 25 Oct. 1785
4) Susan Margaret b. 18 May 1786 m. John FRASER
5) George Frederick b. 30 April 1788 m. Susan BOUTILIER, dau. of John George BOUTILIER
6) James b. 3 Dec. 1791 m. (1) Elizabeth DAUPHINEE and m. 2) Sarah AWALT
7) Joseph b. 5 Oct. 1793 d. young
8) John George b. 3 Dec. 1795 m. Peggy RICHARDSON
9) Jacob b. 1797 m. Hannah DAUPHINEE dau. of John George DAUPHINEE
10) John b. 1800 m. Bridget FLEET
11) Henry b. 1803 m. (1) Amelia UMLAH & m. (2) Isabella McDONALD dau. of Hugh McDONALD
12) Sarah b. 1805 m. James CROUCHER Jr.
13) Barbara m. John UMLAH in 1825

BOUTILIER FAMILY: HENRY

Henry BOUTILIER son of James and Susan Boutilier
Henry BOUTILIER b. 1803 m. (1) Amelia UMLAH

Children:
1) James David b. 25 Dec. 1825
2) Margaret Elizabeth b. 14 Feb. 1827
3) William Henry b. 27 Oct. 1831
4) Joan Amelia b. 18 Mar. 1834 (twin)
5) Mary Jane b. 18 Mar. 1834 (twin)

Henry BOUTILIER b. 1803 m. (2) Isabella MacDONALD
Children:
1) Eleanor b. 21 Mar. 1836
2) James Archibald b. 18 May 1837
3) Peter b. 21 June 1841
4) Isabel b. 1 Sept. 1842
5) Henry b. 14 Oct. 1843
6) Albert b. 7 Dec. 1845
7) Isaac b. 16 July 1848
8) Angeline b. 27 May 1853

BOUTILIER FAMILY:
JAMES ARCHIBALD

James Archibald BOUTILIER, son of Henry and Isabella BOUTILIER
James Archibald BOUTILIER m. Ellen UMLAH
Children:
1) James Henry b. 17 Aug. 1862 m. Mabel BOUTILIER
2) Willis David b. 13 Nov. 1863 m. Lydia BOUTILIER
3) Isabella b. 30 Apr. 1865 m. George FRASER
4) Rebecca Augusta, b. 18 Sept. 1868 m. Foster NAUSS
5) John Isaac b. 27 Sept. 1870 m. Mary ZINCK
6) Mary Amelia b. 15 Oct. 1872 m. Richard DOREY of Hubbards
   Children:
   a) Reid Richard DOREY b. 6 Sept. 1895
   b) Dow Gibson DOREY b. 6 Apr. 1897
   c) Ford Ulric DOREY b. 3 Feb. 1899
   d) Rebecca Alice DOREY b. 13 Oct. 1900
   e) Albert DOREY b. 24 Feb. 1908
7) Margaret Jane b. 5 Feb. 1876 m.. Albert APPLIN
8) Napean Frank b. 28 July 1878 m. Hilda MACDONNELL

(The BOUTILIER Family information was recorded in a family history of the Boutiliers of St. Margaret's Bay put together by Maggie Boutilier.)

DAUPHINEE FAMILY

Jean Christopher DAUPHINEE - bap. 27 Oct. 1757 d. 31 May 1835, m. 1776 to Mary
Elizabeth BOUTILIER b. 1753, d. 24 Oct. 1849 dau. of Jean and Françoise
BOUTILIER

1) Jean George DAUPHINEE - son of Jean Christopher DAUPHINEE b. 20 Oct. 1790 d.
23 Feb. 1867 m. to Susan Ellen MARRYAT from Harrietsfield, NS b. 9 April 1793 d. 12
Dec. 1869

Children:
(a) Mary b. 1813 m. 21 Nov. 1838 to Charles COVEY

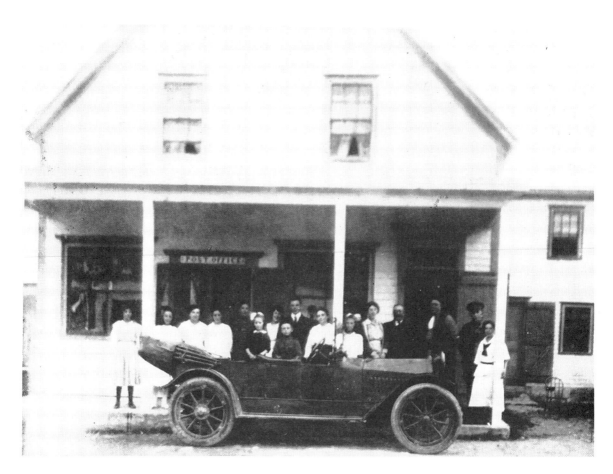

OSWALD DAUPHINEE WITH FAMILY AND HIRED HELP IN FRONT OF GENERAL STORE IN HACKETT'S COVE. 1916
PANS

OSWALD DAUPHINEE'S FAMILY, TAKEN THE ONLY TIME THE WHOLE FAMILY WAS TOGETHER. HIS SON, STANLEY, DIED IN WORLD WAR I AT VIMY RIDGE IN 1917 (SEE APPENDIX). 1916
PANS

DAUPHINEE MEN: LEFT
TO RIGHT, LINDSAY,
OSWALD, GEORGE
(FATHER) AND WILLIAM.
C. 1890

PANS

SARAH DAUPHINEE
(MRS. WILLIAM KEANS)
OF HUBBARDS, ENJOYING
A SUNNY AFTERNOON. C.
1915

PANS

b) Maria b. 14 Jan. 1815 d. 13 Mar. 1874 m. (1) 1832 to James Peter BOUTILIER s/o John Peter and Mary (BURGOYNE) BOUTILIER and m. (2) to James FLOYD

c) Thomas b. 1816 d. 24 Mar. 1882 m. 26 Mar. 1836 to Hannah LANGILLE b. 1811 d. 28 May 1886

d) Helen b. 2 Mar. 1817 d. 26 Dec. 1884 m. to John FADER b. 1807 d. 10 June 1882

e) Susan b. 27 Dec. 1819 d. 16 Apr. 1890 m.(1) 11 Dec. 1839 to Francis BOUTILIER s/o John Peter and Mary BOUTILIER m.(2) to James David DAUPHINEE s/o Fred and Hannah DAUPHINEE

f) Charlotte b. 18 Aug. 1822 m. 27 Jan. 1849 to George Fitzroy CROOK

g) John George b. 19 Feb. 1828 d. 21 Mar. 1901 m. 8 June 1850 to Emily Elizabeth BOUTILIER b. 24 Apr. 1834 d. 21 April 1905 d/o Jacob and Hannah (DAUPHINEE) BOUTILIER. Their children were:

Children:
1) Isabella b. 10 Sept. 1852 m. Joseph FADER
2) Annie m. Frank BOUTILIER
3) John b. 20 Feb. 1857 d. 22 May 1857
4) Thomas Oswald b. 31 Oct. 1858 d. 18 Mar. 1859
5) Hannah Susan b. Nov. 1860 m. Edward CHRISTIE
6) Prudence b. 11 June 1862 m. Henry KERR
7) William b. 20 Oct. 1865 m. Harriet CROSS
8) Oswald b. 9 Oct. 1868 d. 28 Sept. 1927 m. 10 June
     1891 to Clara Angelina GIBBONS
     b. 26 July 1867 d. 4 Dec. 1964

Children od Oswald and Clara DAUPHINEE:

1) Mabel Gertrude b. 29 Aug. 1891 d. 8 July 1985
2) Hazel Edna b. 1 Oct. 1892
3) Cyril Leslie b. 26 Feb. 1894 d. 7 Nov. 1957
4) Annie Florence b. 26 Mar. 1896
5) Stanley Oswald b. 27 Dec. 1897 d. 17 April 1917 at Vimy Ridge
6) George Stewart b. 11 Apr. 1899 d. 10 Feb. 1969
7) Vera Jean b. 7 Sept. 1901 d. 8 Jan. 1952
8) Laura Marjorie b. 17 June 1903
9) Eleanor Gladys b. 27 Nov. 1904
10) Guy Clifford b. 16 July 1906
11) Emily Belle b. 29 Mar. 1908

g) Lindsay b. 4 Nov. 1871 d. 24 Feb. 1965 m. 1 Jan. 1900 to Isabella Sinclaire MUIRHEAD
h) Mary Ann b. 28 Aug. 1831 d. 7 Dec. 1918 m. 26 Feb. 1857 to Charles MASON
i) Isabel b. 6 Sept. 1833 d. 24 Oct. 1911 m. 16 Nov. 1853 to Peter James FADER

DOREY FAMILY

Nehemiah Stamer DOREY of Tantallon (b. 1859 - d. 1936) was the son of John and Susan (CONRAD) DOREY of Fox Point, Lunenburg County m. to Francis Maude (BURGOYNE) Dorey (6. 1839 - d. 1957) dau. of Jacob and Amelia (DAUPHINEE) BURGOYNE.

Children:

1) John Oswald b. 1891 m. Hattie DAUPHINEE
2) Edith May b. 1891 b. 1897
3) Frank Cecil b. 1892 m. Nita TAGGART
4) George Albert b. 1894 m. Anna MARSHALL
5) William b. 1897 m. Annie GIBBONS
6) Everett Franklyn b. 1898 m. Helena GIBBONS
7) Mary Isabella b. 1900 m. Garfield DAUPHINEE
8) Lillian Margaret b. 1902 m. Milton MCDONALD
9) Clifford Arthur b. 1904 m. Shirley HUBLEY
10) Charles Augustus b. 1905 m. Bertha DAUPHINEE
11) Carrie Maude b. 1908 m. Frank GIBBONS
12) Lottie Elsie b. 1911 m. Roy LANAGHAN

Source: Information for Dauphinee and Dorey Family genealogy supplied by Gary Meade, of Head of St. Margaret's Bay

FADER FAMILY:

John Henry FADER Jr. (b. 1848 - d. 1934) was the 5th son of 14 children born to John Henry FADER Sr. (b. 1818 - d. 1894) and Mary Ann MASON (b. 1821 - d. 1894). He m. Annie Rebecca LAPHAM

Children:

1) Blanche b. 1876
2) Stewart b. 1878
3) Lebriton John b. 1880
4) Ansley Welford b. 1882
5) Hazel Annie b. 1883
6) Drucilla Catherine b. 1884
7) Almon Henry b. 1886
8) Weldon Stanley b. 1887
9) Clifford Martell b. 1889
10) Flossie Lillian Beatrice b. 1890
11) Ruby Marie b. 1894
12) Victor Brenton b. 1896
13) Doris Ethel b. 1897
14) Beryl Lapham b. 1898
15) Marjorie Jean b. 1900
16) Franklyn Adair b. 1902

(The FADER family had a farm on a peninsula of land now called Allen Heights, formerly called Oakland Point.)

FRASER FAMILY:

John FRASER b. 1783 in Shelburne County. When 12 years old he stowed away on a ship owned by the Boutilier family of French Village. Married 1803 to Suzanne Margaret BOUTILIER b. 1786 d/o James BOUTILIER

Children:

1) Annie b. 16 Apr. 1810 m. John ISNOR
2) Susan b. 1 Apr. 1811 m. Thomas MAHAR
3) William b. 1 Sept. 1812 m. Bessie MARVIN
4) Barbara b. 29 May 1814
5) Sarah b. 1 Mar. 1816 m. Peter MOSER
6) Elizabeth b. 21 Jan. 1818
7) John b. 3 Apr. 1819 m. 1842 to Hannah MOSER b. 8 Dec. 1824

 Children:

a) Robert b. 1844 m. Jennet Margaret MUNRO
b) John Dallas b. 1846 m. Margaret WRIGHT
c) Angus b. 13 Apr. 1847 m. Lydia
d) Herbert b. 21 Nov. 1849 m. Elizabeth ROBSON

e) Ada (Aunt Madge) b. 1 Mar. 1851

f) Mary Ellen (died young)

g) Jeremiah b. 17 Apr. 1854 m. Annie Maud RICHARDSON

h) George G. b. 4 Mar. 1856 m. Isabella S. BOUTILIER

i) James b. 1861

j) Thomas Edward b. 15 Apr. 1863 m. Eliza HUBLEY

k) Frederick W. b. 3 Apr. 1867 m. Alice MInerva Richardson

l) Charles b. 1869 m. Francis Mary LAWS of England

m) Ernnie b. 1868 m. Helen MARVIN

8) Isabel Jennet b. 6 Mar. 1822 m. William MARVIN

9) James Simon b. 23 Apr. 1826 m. Annie MOSHER

10) Joseph

JAMES ARCHIBALD GARRISON AND WIFE BARBARA (BOUTILIER) IN FRONT OF THEIR HOME IN BOUTILIER'S POINT. C. 1903

PANS

GARRISON FAMILY:

James Archibald GARRISON s/o Harry GARRISON and grandson of Abraham GARRISON a Loyalist, m. in 1860 Barbara Eliza BOUTILIER.

Children:

    1) Alice
    2) Harry
    3) Arthur
    4) Whidden
    5) James
    6) Hibbert
    7) Judidiah
    8) Zilpha (Dolly)
    9) Norman
    10) Lindsay Maxwell b. 1878

BARBARA GARRISON CHURNING BUTTER ON HER DOORSTOOP. C. 1905

PANS

GIBBONS FAMILY:

John Gibbons m. to Amy Fraser PERRY of Roseway, Shelburne County, Nova Scotia.

Children:

1) Wesley Forrester b. 12 Jan. 1862 d. 21 July 1927
2) Elizabeth Richards b. 10 Feb. 1864 d. 1956
3) Alice Moore b. 26 Nov. 1865
4) Clara Angeline b. 26 July 1867 d. 4 Dec. 1964 m. 10 June 1891 to Oswald DAUPHINEE b. 9 Oct. 1868
5) Leslie Mirandola Rand b. 4 Nov. 1870 d. 1 Sept. 1962
6) Fletcher Melbourne b. 7 Oct. 1872 d. in infancy
7) Arthur Augusta b. 9 Dec. 1874 d. Feb. 1963

8) Minerva Theodosia b. 25 Feb. 1876 d. 5 Mar. 1964
9) Herbert Allison b. 12 Sept. 1877 d. 7 Jan. 1962
10) Frank Tupper b. 12 Apr. 1879 d. 1 Sept. 1963

Frank Tupper GIBBONS first moved to Hubbards then to Ingramport.

H U B L E Y   F A M I L Y :

Johann Ulrich HUBLI b. 1719 d. 17 Jan. 1802 came to Nova Scotia in 1751. He married four times, first wife must have died before coming to Nova Scotia. There are no records available. Married (2) 24 Mar. 1752 to Maria Magdalena widow of Bernhard DUTZEL, m. (3) 10 July 1753 to Maria TREFFIAN and m. (4) 3 July 1759 to Barbara LOEW, a widow, b. 1726 d. 24 Apr. 1803. Johann Ulrich HUBLI (HUBLEY) and Barbara LOEW (LOW) had 5 children.
Children: by Barbara LOEW (LOW)
   1) Ferdinand b. 1761 d. 1833 of Northwest Cove, Lunenburg County, NS

GIBBONS FAMILY AND FRIENDS. LEFT TO RIGHT: STANDING, HAROLD GIBBONS, CYRIL DAUPHINEE, MINNIE GIBBONS, BESSIE GIBBONS, FRED FRASER; SITTING, MR. JOHN GIBBONS, MRS. GIBBONS AND GRANDMOTHER. C. 1900

PANS

2) Jacob b. 1762 of Mahone Bay, Lunenburg County, NS

3) John Michael b. 1764 died young

4) George Bernard b. 1769 family at Black Point

5) Johannes b. 1770 d. 1848 of Seabright m. 11 May 1797 to Anna Maria KEELER b. 1773 d. 1871

   Children:

   a) John Jacob b. c. 1798

   b) Ann Elizabeth b. 1799 m. Mr. COLLISHAW

   c) John b. 1800 (an invalid)

   d) George Bernard b. 1802

   e) Catherine b. 1803 d. 1838 m. Mr. MACDONALD

   f) Ferdinand b. 1804

   g) Elizabeth Barbara b. 1806 m. Mr. CARMICHAEL

   h) Alexander b. 1809 d. 1861 m. Jane COMINGOE. He moved from Hubley Settlement (now Seabright) to Hubley and built the Fourteen Mile House

   i) Benjamin

   j) William

   k) Frederick b. 1813 d. 1879

   l) Mary m. Mr. COVEY

Source: Hubley family information supplied by T. Punch, Halifax, NS in 1984.

RICHARDSON FAMILY

Isaac RICHARDSON b. 29 Oct. 1829 d. 16 Jan. 1905, lived in Indian Harbour. He was son of George RICHARDSON (b. 11 June 1796 d. 4 May 1879 who m. 5 Jan. 1816 to Susanna HILTZ b. 14 Oct. 1801 d. 20 May 1864). Isaac m. 12 Jan. 1834 to Ann CORKUM b. 13 April 1834 d. 17 Nov. 1905 the dau. of Peter CORKUM (b. 18 Aug. 1788 d. 3 July 1852 who m. 25 Mar. 1812 to Sophia HUBLEY b. 12 June 1797 d. 13 Aug. 1861). They had nine children.

Children:

   1) Priscilla b. 22 Oct. 1854 d. 26 Apr. 1937 m. 30 Nov. 1880 to Norman COVEY

   2) Joel b. 7 Dec. 1856 d. 28 Dec. 1860

   3) Esrom S. b. 9 Feb. 1859 m. (1) to Mellitta BOUTILIER m. (2) Bessie ALLAN

   4) Isaac Burton b. 1 May 1861 d. 7 Nov. 1918 m. 10 Jan 1895 to Naomi COLLISHAW

   5) George Garfield b. 5 Dec. 1863 d. 19 July 1926 (?)

   6) Lydia A. b. 26 Dec. 1865 d. 1926 m. 24 May 1894 to (1) James COVEY and m. (2) to Arthur ZINCK

   7) Zacharias b. 15 Oct. 1868 d. 10 Oct. _____

   8) Sophia M. b. 4 Mar. 1871 d. 2 June 1877

   9) Thomas J. b. 9 Oct. 1873 d. 7 June 1877

Source: Information provided by Miriam Levy of Indian Harbour in 1987.

THREE MEN FROM
HUBBARDS - AN
UNKNOWN MAN, RICHARD
ELIJAH DOREY AND
CHARLES MCLEAN.
C. 1890

PANS

SHATFORD FAMILY

John Edward SHATFORD was the son of a seaman who had been aboard the British square-rigger *Java* when it was sunk by the American frigate *Constitution* during the War of 1812. He had settled in Fox Point after two years in a Virginia prisoner-of-war camp. John Edward SHATFORD came to Hubbards in 1860 and operated a successful general store business, was in the Municipal Council for 20 years and a County Warden for 10 years. He was the local postmaster from 1872 - 1887 at a salary of $24.50 per year. His sons, all very successful in business, were:
   1) Sidney Smith SHATFORD
   2) Jefferson Davis SHATFORD
   3) John Franklyn SHATFORD (Frank)
   4) A. Wellesley SHATFORD
   5) Alma Hastings SHATFORD
Source: *Bay News*, November 1985

CECIL LEVY (SITTING)
AND HIS BROTHER
NORMAN LEVY
(STANDING) –
GRANDSONS OF DANIEL
AND HANNAH LEVY OF
HACKETT'S COVE. C.
1914

PANS

SNAIR FAMILY

(also Schner, Schnare)

John George SCHNARE b. 1802 in Chester, Nova Scotia d. Queensland, was s/o John SCHNER and Mary Elizabeth MORASH of East Chester. He m. Mary Elizabeth ZINCK, had a son John David SCHNARE.

John David SCHNARE b. 1847 in Queensland, NS d. 13 Dec. 1930 in Queensland, m. (1) 20 Dec. 1866 to Angeline SMELTZER in Hubbards, NS, m. (2) 4 Nov. 1876 to Louisa BRIGLEY, m. (3) 4 Nov. 1880 to Annie MANUEL.

Children:

1) Freeman b. 1867 in Queensland, NS d. 1949 m. 1893 to Lottie Grace MANUEL. 7 children
    a) Firman Halstrod b. 1897
    b) Nellie b. 1898

UNKNOWN LADY FROM FRENCH VILLAGE. (PHOTO COPIED FROM TINTYPE.) C. 1880

PANS

c) Lawrence b. 1910
d) Laura b. 1905
e) Jeremiah b. 1912
f) Marion
g) Elizabeth
2) Oscar (drowned)
3) Warden b. 1896 d. 1948
4) Frank
5) Sidney d. 8 Jan. 1923
6) Allen
7) Maude
8) George
9) Robert m. Charlotte SELIG
10) Helena m. Charles SNAIR
Source: Family Group Sheets from Bonnie Slauenwhite of Ingramport, NS.

TWO CHILDREN ON WHARF OVERLOOKING BAY IN GLEN MARGARET. C. 1930

PANS

SAILBOATS IN INDIAN HARBOUR CATCHING THE WIND. C. 1920

PANS

The Public Record

Name Changes

IN ST. MARGARET'S BAY

These are a few examples showing how the spelling of names have changed over the centuries. Some names may have more than one spelling.

Then	Now
Ewald	Awalt
Bautillea	Boutilier
Coulen	Coolen/Cooling
Dauphin	Dauphinee
Gorckum	Corkum
Dawsey	Dawson
Kock	Cook
Hemlock/Humlah	Umlah
Theil	Deal
Uelshe	Hilchie
Lankert	Longard
Bubickhoffer	Publicover
Rahfuss	Rafuse
Schlagentweit	Slaunwhite
Phelon	Whealon
Jung	Young
Darez	Dorey
Westhoffer	Westhaver
Schnare	Snair

A Boutilier's Cove scene in Hackett's Cove. 1925

PANS

A scene showing Hackett's Cove. c. 1920

PANS

A scene showing Glen Margaret. c. 1920

PANS

Return of Settlers

at St. Margaret's Bay 27 June 1817

Name	Men	Women	Children	Servants
Croucher, James	1			
Croucher, John	1	1	1	1
Manville, Peter	1	1	2	2
Keyser, John	1	1	2	
Troop, William	1			
Dobben, Richard	1			
Kayser, Jacob	1			
Croucher, Thomas	1			
Freeman, John	1	1	4	
Richardson, John	1		3	
Covey, James	1	1	4	
Woods, Richard	1	1		1
Andrews, Jacob	1	1	2	
Bowie, William	1	1		
Covey, William	1	1	2	
Grono, Christopher	1	1	6	
Grono, George	1	1	6	
Scott, James	1	1	4	
Boutilier, James	1	1	4	2
Boutilier, James Jr.	1	1	1	
Rooder, Michael	1	1	5	
Wambolt, Peter	1	1	4	
Troop, James	1	1	2	
Moser, John	1	1	2	
Trueman, Thomas	1	1	2	
Potts, John	1	1	5	
Isner, William	1	1	3	
Duffiney, Christopher	1	1	8	
Boutilier, Joseph	1	1	7	
Boutilier, Joseph Jr.	1	1	1	
Whynot, Michael	1	1	4	
Slawenwight, Jacob Sr.	1	1	1	
Slawenwight, Martin	1	1	4	
Boutilier, James Frederick	1	1		

Name	Men	Women	Children	Servants
Boutilier, John	1	1	2	
Jollymore, George	1	1	5	
Boutilier, George	1	1	7	
Cornelius, Daniel	1		3	
Boutilier, James	1	1	4	
Dorey, George	1	1		
Dorey, James	1	1	2	
Slawenwight, Frederick	1	1	6	2
Bridley, John	1	1	3	
Duffiney, John	1	1	3	5
Thompson, William	1			
Shupley, Henry	1	1	1	
Schwartz, Christopher	1	1	1	
Westhaver, John	1	1	2	1
Harnish, Jacob	1	1	8	1
Harnish, George	1	1	8	
Harnish, Gottlib	1	1		1
Sawler, Henry	1	1	4	1
Coolen, Joseph	1	1	4	1
Jollymore, Christopher	1	1	4	
Dominy, William	1	1	3	
Jollymore, James	1	1		
Noonan, Patrick	1	1	4	1
Dorey, George Sr.	1	1	4	
Noonan, James	1			
Hollahan, Thomas	1	1		4
Mahon, Patrick	1			
Withein, William	1	1		
Carrol, John	1		1	
Hickey, James	1	1		2
Simms, Charles	1	1	5	
Isner, John	1	1	2	
Isner, George	1	1	3	
Fraser, John	1	1	5	
Moore, John	1	1	4	
Marvin, John	1	1	3	
Ranfro, Alexander	1	1		
McGrath, John	1	1	6	
Warrington, George	1	1		
Emblee, John	1		5	
Hubley, John Sr.	1	1	6	

Name	Men	Women	Children	Servants
Hubley, John Jr.	1	1	6	
McDonald, Archibald	1	1	1	
Boutilier, Christopher	1	1	53	
Boutilier, John	1	1	3	
Boutilier, John F.	1	1	4	
Boutilier, Frederick	1	1	3	
Dugle, John	1	1	2	
Duffiney, Frederick	1	1	3	
Duffiney, John	1	1	3	
Duffiney, John George	1	1		2
Holland, Thomas (schoolmaster)	1			
Boutilier, Frederick	1	1	7	
Burgoyne, Jacob	1	1	1	
Boutilier, Peter	1	1	3	2
Boutilier, David	1	1	8	
Boutilier, John George	1		2	
Kiddy, William	1	1	6	1
Boutilier, George	1	1	3	
Boutilier, John	1	1	3	
Duffeney, James	1	1	3	
Totals	99	85	290	32

In all a total of 506 people

Source: PANS, R.G. 20 Series 'C', Vol. 88, Item #174
Terrence M. Punch, 1979

List of Scholars

AT THE PEGGY'S COVE SCHOOL
DISTRICT: IN 1848

Teacher - James Wilson

Boys	Age	Girls	Age
Holmwood, Henry	8	Garrison, Isabella	10
Holmwood, John	6	Garrison, Elizabeth	15
Garrison, Elias	18	Daubin, Amelia	14
Garrison, George	13	Croucher, Nancy	13
Garrison, Henry	8	Daubin, Sarah	10
Garrison, William	6	McGratch, Jane	13
Croucher, Amos	11	McGratch, Sarah	9
McGratch, David	15	Manuel, Ann	9
Keizer, Charles	14	Crooks, Magdalene	14
Manuel, William	8	Crooks, Eliza	14
Manuel, John	6	Crooks, Matilda	7
Massey, Samuel	23	Croucher, Susan	9
Crooks, John	13	Moore, Elizabeth	13
Crooks, Richard	8		
Crooks, James	11		
Crooks, Westley	6		
Crooks, William	12		
Crooks, Henry	8		
Wilson, Gufus	8		

Subjects Taught
Bible and Testament
English Reader
Spelling
Primer
Geography
Arithmetic

Source: PANS RG 14 Vol. 26 1848
(Names are recorded as they were written in 1848)

RESIDENTS OF

Indian Harbour

IN 1866

Allen, Christopher Sr.
Allen, Christopher Jr.
Allen, Joseph
Allen, John
Boutilier, Fred
Boutilier, John
Covey, Thomas
Covey, William
Covey, Charles
Covey, Elias
Covey, Ben
Covey, John
Corkum, Ben
Croucher, Sam
Fredericks, George
Graves, Isaac
Garrison, John
Johnson, William
Johnson, Thomas
Johnson, John
Johnson, Cyrus
Lantz, Joe
Manuel, Mike
Manuel, Peter
Richardson, John
Richardson, Samuel
Richardson, Charles
Richardson, James Jr.
Richardson, Daniel
Richardson, John
Richardson, Edward
Richardson, Joseph
Richardson, George
Richardson, James Sr.
Richardson, W. Daniel
Shatford, C. James
Wambold, John
Zwicker, Ben

Source: PANS RG 14 Vol. 27 #107 1866

Assessment Roll

FOR DISTRICT #12
(NOW TANTALLON)

Recorded on December 17, 1896

The following list of names were sent by Isaac J. Boutilier to the Municipal Clerk, W.H. Wiswell, at the Municipality of Halifax:

Tanner, Jeremiah
Frederick, Charles
Frederick, John
Longard, Stephen
Longard, John
Longard, Levi
Dauphiney, George
Dauphiney, Edward
Dauphiney, Elias
Dauphiney, Judson
Dauphiney, Benjamin
Dauphiney, Nathaniel
Dauphiney, Isaac
Dauphiney, Adolphus
Boutilier, Frederick J.
Boutilier, Peter I.
Boutilier, Isaac J.
Boutilier, Samuel J.
Boutilier, Angus J.
Boutilier, Lewis J.
Boutilier Amos J.
Boutilier, Peter C.
Burgoyne, Jacob
Mason, Edward
Smith, George
Smith, Stephen
Smith, Joseph
Smith, John C.
Slaunwhite, Rhuben (?)
Young, Jeremiah
Dorey, Nemiah

Source: PANS RG 14 Vol. 27 #309 1896

Business Directory

Adams, H.	Teacher at Hubbart's Cove
Boutilier, P.G.	Farmer
Bissett, W.	Trader and Way office Keeper
Culp, G.	House Carpenter
Cooling, W.	Fisherman and Farmer, Shad Bay
Croucher, J. (Senior)	J.P. Shopkeeper and Farmer
Dauphinee, D.	Fisherman and farmer
Dauphinee, G.	Inn-keeper and Farmer
Dauphinee, J.L.	Farmer
Duncan, John	Lumberman, Ingram River
Eisenhaur, W.	Fisherman and Farmer
Fraser, W.	Farmer and Fishing Business
Fader, J.H.	Fisherman and Farmer
Fralick, J.	Fisherman and Farmer
Garrison, A.	Fisherman and Farmer
Hubley, B.M.	Mason and Brocklayer
Hubley, C. Sr.	Coaster
Hornish, J.	Fisherman
Isener, P.	Fisherman and Farmer
Isener, J.	Farmer
Lantz, J.	Shoemaker and Shopkeeper
Mason, M.	Fisherman's Inn
Mason, S.J.	School Teacher
McLean, N.C.	McLean's Hotel, Hubbart's Cove
Mason, F.	Boot and Shoemaker and Farmer
McLean, Charles	Fisherman and Farmer
Mason, S.J.	Artist and Farmer
McDonald, A.	Blacksmith
Mahar, T.	Trader, Fisherman and Farmer
Munro, C.	Farmer
Nickerson, J.S.	Mariner
Pace, W.T.	Boatbuilder and Fisherman
Shatford, J.E.	J.P. and Shopkeeper
Shatford, S.	Trader and Coaster
Webber, A.	Millowner, Lumberman and Coaster

Business Directory

PEGGY'S COVE - 1864

Crooks, John Sr.	J.P. and Fisherman
Crooks, William Sr.	Dealer in Dry Goods and Groceries and Fishing Business
Milbury, Seth	Fishing Business
Daubin, James	Fishing Business
Daubin, Richard	Fishing Business
Garrison, George	Fishing Business
Innes, Robert	Fishing Business
Keizer, Charles	Fishing Business
Massey, Samuel	Fishing Business
Manuel, James	Fishing Business
Crooks, John	Fisherman
Innis, John	Fisherman

Source: A.F. Church Map of Halifax County - 1864

FRENCH VILLAGE BEFORE ROAD WAS PAVED. C. 1930

PANS

St. Margaret's Bay

In 1845 a Halifax newspaper, *The Register* published poetry written by either its staff or readers. Since the newspaper does not mention who the poet is, we must assume that the following poem was written by someone who enjoyed visiting the Bay and was impressed by its beauty. The original poem contains five stanzas, two of which are reprinted here:

Wild Scenes of Nova Scotia

A SERIES OF STANZAS NO. 3
ST. MARGARET'S BAY

From thy soft sky bower come awake, gentle breeze!
And waft me away from those deep, dashing seas,
To where verdure and blossom enliven the day
And the winds bear sweet scents to the wild woods away.
To the shore and the shallow
I now bid adieu
And welcome the scene
That is open to view —
A bright sheet of waters
As dazzling and fair,
As ever was fanned
By the sweet summer air

Up — up through the forest it winds in its pride
With inlets so pleasing and basins so wide,
Where swift glancing fishes leap out to the Sun
Bright'ning all the fair wave til the daylight is done.
And many an Isle
Is asleep on its breast
Shadowed over with pines,
And in green wilderness dress'd
Sequestered retreats
Where the limpet's light lay
Makes a heav'n all day long
Of this beautiful Bay!

Source: *The Register* 1845, p. 281 - PANS Reel #8150

Pioneer Cemetery

The following list consists of the information recorded from the 29 headstones which are still standing in this small cemetery in French Village:

1) DOREY, Edith May, d. 8 Apr. 1897, age 6, dau. of Nehemiah and Fannie Dorey
2) DRISCOLL, Harriet, d. 16 Feb. 1889, age 33
3) BOUTILIER, Elizabeth, d. 15 Oct. 1901, age 79, wife of Benjamin
4) BOUTILIER, Benjamin F., d. 5 Dec. 1898, age 50
5) LONGARD, Edward R., 1891-1956 and Edith F., wife 1894-1963
6) MASON, Hannah, 1867-1964
7) MASON, George T., 1900-1944
8) MASON, Stanley L., 1898-1944
9) MASON, Lillian, d. 30 May 1891, age 1 day
   MASON, Neil A., d. 5 Nov. 1911, age 3 mos.
10) MASON, J. Edward, 1862-1919 and Isaac, 1909-1913
11) HUBLEY, Gordon F., d. 3 Jan. 1921, age 34 "husband"
12) HUBLEY, Daniel, d. 7 Dec. 1883, age 66 and Maria, wife, d. 19 Mar. 1876, age 45
13) HUBLEY, Levi, d. 25 Oct. 1920, age 67
14) Peter Christopher, d. 22 Jan. 1828, age 18 yr. 2 mos., son of Christopher and Sarah DAUPHINEE
15) Joseph Christopher, d. 19 Jan. 1828, age 25 yr. 2 mos. 18 days, son of Christopher and Sarah DAUPHINEE
16) James C., d. 12 Jan. 1828, age 22 yr. 10 mos., son of Christopher and Sarah DAUPHINEE
17) MCGOWAN, Sarah Jane, d. June 1901, 28, wife of James
18) DAUPHINEE, Susan M., 1829-1941, wife of Adolphus
19) DAUPHINEE, Stephen, 1833-1889
    Sarah A., wife 1839-1922
    Samuel J., 1875-1910
    Stanley M., 1877-1895
    Angus, 1883-1883
20) BOUTILIER, Louisa M., d. 28 Mar. 1911, age 48, dau. of Isaac J. and Louisa
21) MCDONALD, Allen, 1820-18 Apr. 1886
    Lucy, wife, 31 Oct., 1841-25 Feb. 1896
22) SMITH, Benjamin, d. 9 Apr. 1916, age 43
23) SMITH, Margaret, d. 17 Feb. 1911, age 37, wife of Benjamin
24) JOHNSON, J. Edward, d. 1 Aug. 1920, age 80
    HAMILTON, Georgina, his wife, 1851-1935
    COLP, Frederick, Frederick R. d. 1 Apr. 1914, age 17
25) MCDONALD, Henry, d. 25 Dec. 1895, age 21 yr. 2 mos.
26) MCDONALD, Archibald, d. 15 March 1851, age 64
27) MCDONALD, Archibald, 24 Nov. 1821 - 25 Feb, 1875
28) LAING, Jessie, d. 4 Mar. 1911, age 82, wife of Archibald MCDONALD
29) MCDONALD, Harold, infant son of George and Maude

Source: *Bay News*, May 1984, p. 12, written by Gary Meade

Bibliography

PRIMARY SOURCES:

Public Archives of Nova Scotia

Library
1) V/F Vol. 246 #26 *A Visitor's Guide to St. Margaret's Bay.*
2) HE N85 SM5 1749-1815 p. 170, 172 "Coaches". *Transportation and Commerce in Nova Scotia.*
3) F80 C16R 1904 p. 291 *Report of the Public Archives of Canada.*
4) AK B12 St2 1851 Anglican Church *The Report for the Society of Propagation of the Gospel.*
5) F100 H13 V.2. *History of Nova Scotia* v. 11,p. 25-25.
6) J104 K3R29. *Nova Scotia Power Corporation* by T.C. Haliburton. 1920-1944p. 881
7) Inns - micro N938, 1920-30, p. 38-40 *Report of the Provincial Museums.*
8) L764 1995 PANS *Thomas Mahar of Glen Margaret.*
9) F90 N85S Vol. 13 - 1913-1914. *Churches.*

Record Groups - RG
1) RG 1 Vol. 444 DOC.1-1793 *List of Males in St. Margaret's Bay.*
2) RG 5 Series GP Misc. A Vol. 4 1861 *Biography on John Fraser Sr..*
3) RG 5 Series P Vol. 49 #78 *Request for a Lighthouse.*
4) RG 5 Series P Vol. 121 #24 1826 *Fishery Regulations.*
5) RG 7 Vol. 41 1859 *Union Hall Company*, Alex Hubley.
6) RG 5 Series P Vol. 90 #150 1823 *Petition for Roads*
7) RG 5 Series P Vol. 74 #16 1843 *Petition for Roads*
8) RG 5 Series P Vol. 75 #21, 37 1849 *Petition for Roads*
9) RG 1 Vol. 430 Doc. 26 1/2 1786 *Indian Land Grant.*
10) RG 5 Vol. 49 #78 Series P 1860 *Lighthouses.*
11) RG 5 Series P. Vol. 72 #83 *Schools*
12) RG 5 Series P. Vol. 23-27 1828,1834, 1840 *PANS School Papers.*

Manuscript Groups

1) MG 4 Vol. 105 *Harris Notes Vol. XII, from Church Records*
2) MG 100 Vol. 16 #16 1849 *Orange Lodge*
3) MG 3 Vol. 6190 *Family Store - Fish*
4) MG 3 #643 1915-1922 *Business Papers - Fader Ledger*
5) MG 1 #1059A 1572-1953 *Croucher and Other Families.*
6) MG 100 Vol. 217 #15 1839 *Description Of St. Margaret's Bay*
7) MG 100 Vol. 54 #36 1884-1890 *Community and Families*
8) MG 9 Vol. 46 p. 106 1823 *Baptist Organized - Churches By the Sea* by Allen Gibson
9) MG 1 Vol. 1719 # 1 1890s *Fishery Regulations Decline*

NEWSPAPERS

Acadian recorder
Bay News
Chronicle Herald
Halifax Herald
Mail Star
Novascotian
The Register

Appendix

East River School 1899 - Page 28

Maud Slauenwhite	- Back right
Wesley Slauenwhite	- Second from right
Alice Dorey	- Back row left
Mary Mason	- Back row second from left
Almida Brunswick	- Back row second from right

Lawson Slauenwhite
Clifford Slauenwhite
Amanda Boutilier
Ellen Slauenwhite
Hannah Hurshman
Offil Mason

Ken Morrison	- First teacher
Miss Thompson	- Second teacher

Bottom row
Gladys Slauenwhite   - Third from left

Back row
_____ Slauenwhite   - Fourth in from left

Back row   - Fifth in from left
Mabel Boutilier

Class Picture - Head of St. Margaret's Bay - St. James School - Page 29

October 1939

Teacher George Selig

Back Row: Sheridan Boutilier, Howard Rhyno, James Christie, Marion Christie, Pauline Fader, Marjorie Boutilier, Jack Tupper, Doris Frellick (Fralick), Hanna Boutilier,

Middle Row: Ted Dorey, Marjorie Cook, Lillian Mason, Betty Dunlop, Violet Langille, Dorothy Rhyno, Jean Tupper, Eleanor Boutilier, Opal Fader, Audrey Dunlop.

Front Row: Gordon Boutilier, Darrell Mason, Laurie Dorey, Dawson Dunlop, Victoria Rhyno, Arthur Dauphinee, Leslie Christie, Elmo Tupper.

Hubbards Cove School 1914 - Page 31

Half of Class Picture, from top right: Fred Dauphinee, Herbert MacLean, Gerald Trueman, Eddie Conrad, Edna MacLean, Avon Jollimore, Gladys Huskins, Austin Jollimore, Albert Dorey, Beryl Colp, Geraldine Conrad, Robert Norwood, Amos Schwartz, Frank Norwood, Alfie Huskins, Miss Langille (teacher), Eddie Dauphinee, Ruth Dauphinee, Kash Colp, Jack MacLean, Carl Colp. Thelma Jollimore, Gwen Schwartz, Allan Dauphinee, May Truman.

1939 Tantallon Canadians - Page 78

Back row, left to right: Gary Hurshman, Marsman Jollimore, Harvy Hurshman, Colin Hurshman, Malcolm Seaboyer, _____ MacDonald, Harold Miller.

Front row, left to right: Arnold Croft, George Nash, Ira Swallow, Percy Jollimore, Vincent Whiting, Charlie Balch.

Hubbards Tuna c. 1950 - Page 79

Back row, left to right: George Mills, Jack Miller, John MacLean, Albert Dorey, Gippy Dominy, John Schwartz, Lawrence Winters, Gordie Conrad, Harry Coolen.

Front Row: Herbert Dorey, Tom Dorey, Murdoch Miller, Arnold Dorey, Bobby Trueman, Eddie Porter, Buzz Shankel, Dan Dorey, Billy Blakney.

The Dauphinee Family in 1916 - Page 106

Top row: left to right, Ann, Vera, Eleanor, Mabel, Clara, Cyril, Hazel, Stan.
Front row: left to right, Laura, George, Guy, Oswald, Belle.